GLUTEN
FREE
BAKING

Michael McCamley

GLUTEN FREE BAKING

Just as delicious – just as easy

First published in 2012
LOVE FOOD is an imprint of Parragon Books Ltd

Parragon
Queen Street House
4 Queen Street
Bath BA1 1HE, UK

LOVE FOOD and the accompanying heart device is a registered trade mark of Parragon Books Ltd in
Australia, the UK, USA, India and the EU.

www.parragon.com/lovefood

ISBN: 978-1-4454-9826-3

Printed in China

Recipes by Michael McCamley
Nutritionist Fiona Hunter
Photography by Noel Murphy
Home economy by Jane Lawrie
Design by Lexi L'Esteve

"For my Mother Annie (1929-1989) who inspired me to achieve."

Notes for the Reader
This book uses both metric and imperial measurements. Follow the same units of measurement
throughout; do not mix metric and imperial. All spoon measurements are level: teaspoons are assumed
to be 5 ml, and tablespoons are assumed to be 15 ml. Unless otherwise stated, milk is assumed to be
full fat, eggs and individual vegetables are medium, and pepper is freshly ground black pepper. Unless
otherwise stated, all root vegetables should be washed in plain water and peeled prior to using.

Garnishes, decorations and serving suggestions are all optional and not necessarily included in the
recipe ingredients or method. Any optional ingredients and seasoning to taste are not included in the
nutritional analysis.

The times given are an approximate guide only. Preparation times differ according to the techniques
used by different people and the cooking times may also vary from those given. Optional ingredients,
variations or serving suggestions have not been included in the time calculations.

Recipes using raw or very lightly cooked eggs should be avoided by infants, the elderly, pregnant
women, convalescents and anyone suffering from an illness. Pregnant and breastfeeding women are
advised to avoid eating peanuts and peanut products. Sufferers from nut allergies should be aware that
some of the ready-made ingredients used in the recipes in this book may contain nuts. Always check the
packaging before use.

Contents

Introduction

What is Gluten?

Gluten is a mixture of two proteins, gliadin and glutenin, that is found in wheat, rye and barley and ingredients derived from these cereals. When the grain is milled, it is the gluten which gives the flour its elasticity. The majority of people can eat gluten without any implications or long term adverse effects, however it can cause mild to severe problems for individuals with coeliac disease or gluten intolerance. The difference between coeliac disease and gluten intolerance/sensitivity is very confusing; however, one thing is certain, once a diagnosis has been made, a gluten-free diet is the universal treatment for all.

Coeliac Disease (Spelt 'Celiac' in Some Countries)

Pronounced 'see–liac', coeliac disease is commonly regarded as a food allergy or intolerance, however it is actually an autoimmune disease caused by eating gluten. People with coeliac disease make antibodies against gluten so even a small amount can trigger an immune reaction in people with the condition. Eating gluten damages the lining of the small intestine and other parts of the body may be affected in the long term. Small finger-like projections (villi) line the small intestine and they play a significant role in food digestion. When the villi are damaged and inflamed, they are unable to absorb food properly, this means that the food and nutrients are not properly digested which often causes diarrhoea, malnutrition and other health problems. If coeliac disease is left undiagnosed or if a gluten-free diet is not adhered to following a diagnosis, those with the disease have an increased risk of developing other associated diseases. These include osteoporosis, lymphoma and other autoimmune diseases such as type 1 diabetes, thyroid disease, rheumatoid arthritis, inflammatory bowel disease, Sjögren's syndrome and lupus.

Who Can Get Coeliac Disease?

The cause of coeliac disease is unknown; however, it is thought to be a combination of genetic and environmental factors. If a close family member – for example a brother, sister, parent or child – has been diagnosed then there is a 1 in 10 chance of having coeliac disease. Although approximately 1 in 100 people are thought to have coeliac disease, many are undiagnosed or misdiagnosed as having other types of digestive conditions. Research has shown that the average length of time it takes for a confirmed diagnosis is approximately 13 years. Coeliac disease can develop at any age and for many years it was believed to be a childhood disease that you could grow out of; it is most frequently diagnosed, however, between the ages of 40 to 60 years old. Contrary to common belief, coeliac disease affects all ethnic groups and is found in Europe and North America, as well as in South America, Southern Asia, North Africa and the Middle East. It is most commonly found in countries where wheat plays a large part in the everyday diet.

Symptoms

There are many indicators for coeliac disease, but as people have a unique mix of symptoms, it is often very difficult to pinpoint coeliac disease as the cause. Many of the symptoms mimic or are similar to other diseases, such as Irritable Bowel Syndrome, so it can take years to obtain an accurate diagnosis. The symptoms can vary from person to person and can include one or a combination of the following:

- recurrent gastrointestinal symptoms, such as nausea, vomiting and diarrhoea
- excessive flatulence, and/or constipation
- persistent stomach pain, cramping or bloating
- iron, vitamin B12 or folic acid deficiency
- tiredness
- headaches
- weight loss (but not in all cases)
- mouth ulcers
- hair loss (alopecia)
- skin rash (dermatitis herpetiformis, DH)
- tooth enamel problems
- osteoporosis
- depression and anxiety
- infertility or repeated miscarriages
- joint and/or bone pain
- neurological problems such as ataxia and neuropathy.

Symptoms in babies and young children can also include:
- a bloated tummy
- muscle wasting in the arms and legs
- irritability
- failure to gain or lose weight.

Diagnosis

The first step to diagnosis is discussing the symptoms with a doctor. If your doctor suspects you have coeliac disease, he or she will perform a careful physical examination and will discuss your medical history with you. A blood test should then be carried out in order to detect the presence of antibodies which are produced in response to digested gluten. Your doctor may arrange further tests to detect nutritional deficiencies, such as a blood test to detect iron levels as anaemia can often occur with coeliac disease. A stool sample may be tested to detect fat in the stool, as coeliac disease prevents fat from being absorbed from food. The doctor should then organise a referral to a gastroenterologist for a gut biopsy to test the villi of the small intestine for damage. In a biopsy, the doctor inserts an endoscope (a thin, hollow tube) through your mouth and into the small intestine, and takes a sample of the small intestine with an instrument to examine under a microscope. This is the best way to confirm if you have coeliac disease. More recently, home testing kits for coeliac disease have become available over the counter and online but any results should be discussed and confirmed by your doctor.

Treatment

Coeliac disease cannot be cured; therefore, when a positive diagnosis is confirmed, the only treatment to enable repair of the small intestine and to alleviate the symptoms is to embark on a complete gluten-free diet. This requires considerable support and information. After diagnosis a referral for a consultation with a dietitian should be made, where advice and diet sheets for following a complete gluten-free diet will be given. If tests have shown that nutrient levels are low, vitamins and minerals may be recommended. Following a strict gluten-free diet will reduce the risk of osteoporosis, cancer and associated autoimmune diseases.

False Negative Tests

Many people have negative results to the tests for coeliac disease, however they still suffer from the same symptoms whenever gluten is digested. In this case, they may have had false negative tests. In order to ensure that they do not have false negative tests for coeliac disease they need to continue to eat gluten until the tests have been completed. Abstaining from foods containing gluten will prevent the immune system from producing the antibodies needed for detection in the blood test. Abstaining from gluten prior to the biopsy may also cause the villi in the small intestine to show signs of repair making it difficult for the gastroenterologist to make a conclusive diagnosis of coeliac disease.

Non-Coeliac Gluten Intolerance

If, however, genuine negative test results for coeliac disease are received and symptoms are still being experienced, a person may be suffering from Non-Coeliac Gluten Intolerance. As it shares many of the characteristics of coeliac disease such as bowel problems, tiredness and depression, it is possible that a misdiagnosis can be made. Non-Coeliac Gluten Intolerance is thought to affect approximately 15 per cent of the world's population, the majority of which are still undiagnosed or misdiagnosed. As there are no medical tests to confirm a diagnosis, the only definitive way to treat it is to follow a complete gluten-free diet for a few weeks and then to reintroduce gluten into the diet. If the symptoms return after digestion of gluten, then a Non-Coeliac Gluten Intolerance can be confirmed and a complete gluten-free diet will need to be followed in order to feel well.

Wheat Allergy

Having a wheat allergy differs from having coeliac disease. An allergic reaction to wheat will usually appear within minutes or hours after eating wheat or foods containing wheat, whereas in coeliac disease the symptoms can differ and take longer to develop.

Symptoms of wheat allergy may include one or a combination of the following:
• difficulty breathing, wheezing, coughing or a runny nose
• eczema, hives or other skin rashes
• itchy, red, swollen or watery eyes
• abdominal pain
• nausea, diarrhoea and/or vomiting
• swelling of the lips, tongue or face
• a severe, systemic allergic reaction known as anaphylaxis which is a serious life-threatening condition which requires immediate medical treatment.

The majority of gluten-free products are suitable for those with a wheat allergy although sometimes only

the gluten is removed in the manufacturing process. Therefore, it is always necessary to use caution and check labels carefully.

Dermatitis Herpetiformis

Dermatitis herpetiformis (also referred to as DH) is a blistering skin condition related to coeliac disease, however it is much rarer. It is characterised by extremely itchy bumps and blisters which arise on normal or reddened skin and is most often found on the scalp, shoulders, buttocks, elbows and knees. Like coeliac disease, it involves antibodies and intolerance to gluten. There is a genetic disposition for this disease and it often affects more males than females. Diagnosis involves examining the skin for immunoglobulin A (IgA) and if found, normal testing for coeliac disease is used to confirm the condition. It too is controlled by following a complete gluten-free diet.

Lactose Intolerance and the Association with Coeliac Disease

Lactose is broken down by an enzyme called lactase, which is found in the lining of the small intestine. When the lining is damaged it does not make enough lactase so lactose intolerance can occur. However, once a gluten-free diet is introduced the small intestine is allowed to heal and the normal breakdown of lactose returns. Therefore, lactose intolerance is usually a temporary problem. It is important that a discussion with a dietitian takes place before eliminating lactose from a diet as this will reduce the calcium intake.

Gluten-free and Hidden Gluten

Once diagnosed and following a gluten-free diet, many people may start to feel better almost immediately and continue to improve as their damaged small intestine is repaired and they remain gluten-free. It is important to note that it can take some time for this to occur. There are some who cannot understand why the gluten-free diet is not working for them. The simple answer to this is that hidden gluten can be found in the most unsuspecting of food and sources and so gluten can unknowingly be being digested. As gluten is most commonly found in flour, removing products such as bread, cakes and biscuits from a diet is perceived by many as following a gluten-free diet; however, this is not the case. Gluten is used in many processed products and is hidden in everyday foods. Coeliacs should avoid wheat, rye, barley

and spelt. Although oats contain gluten, it is uncertain whether they should be avoided by coeliacs as oat gluten is from a different family of grains. However, because it is difficult to prevent cross-contamination by wheat in the production process, coeliacs are advised to avoid oats unless it is stated that they are gluten-free. Coeliacs should also be careful when a product states that it is wheat-free, as this does not necessarily mean that it is gluten-free. It is always better to be safe than sorry, so if you are not sure if a product is gluten-free it is better to avoid it.

Today new labelling legislation has made it much easier for coeliacs when purchasing gluten-free products. Products may now only be labelled as gluten-free if the product has less than 20 parts per million of gluten. Companies that produce and package food in the UK must legally have an ingredients list. The manufacturer must therefore state if wheat, rye, oats and barley have been used in their product. Ingredients which have been made from cereals which contain gluten such as glucose syrup, maltodextrin and distilled ingredients are now processed to remove the gluten so are, therefore, gluten-free. Although allergy boxes are not a legal requirement, some manufacturers have begun to use them in recent years. If an allergy box is used on a product it is still necessary to check that it is suitable for your requirements. Today the Food Standards Agency provides guidance to manufacturers with regards to the term 'May Contain'. Manufacturers may use this term on their labelling if they feel that there is a risk that their product may have been contaminated by gluten. Only companies which specialise in producing gluten-free food products are able to use the term 'Gluten-free' or 'Suitable for Coeliacs' on their labelling. Other countries are also establishing new laws and legislation with regards to the labelling of gluten-free products.

Gluten-free Foods

The following foods are all gluten-free:

- meat and poultry

- fish and shellfish

- beans and pulses

- dairy products (milk, cream, cheese and natural yogurt)

- fresh vegetables

- fresh fruit

- eggs

- corn and cornmeal (maize/sweetcorn)

- fats (including butter, margarine and oil)

- rice and wild rice

- rice noodles

- soya and plain tofu

- nuts and seeds

- sugar and honey

- treacle, golden syrup and maple syrup

- vanilla essence and extract

- fresh herbs and spices

- tomato purée

- fresh and dried yeast

- jams and marmalades

- vinegars

- spirits (including whiskey and malt whiskey), wine, champagne, port, sherry, liqueurs and cider.

Hidden Ingredients on Food Labels

On food labels these items may contain gluten:

- wheat/wholewheat
- wheat bran
- wheat germ
- wheat starch
- barley/scotch barley
- bran
- breadcrumbs
- bulgar
- cereal extract
- couscous
- farina
- flour
- wholemeal flour
- wheat flour
- modified starch
- rolled oats
- oatmeal
- rusk
- rye flour
- semolina
- spelt
- kamut
- vegetable protein
- vegetable gum
- vegetable starch.

Hidden Gluten in Foods

The following foods may contain gluten, however, there are gluten-free alternatives to many:

- communion wafers
- commercial ice creams
- frozen yogurts
- cheese spreads
- sour cream
- non-dairy creamer
- custard
- ketchup and some sauces
- dry-roasted nuts
- licorice
- sweets and confectionary
- crisps
- canned baked beans

- canned or packet soups
- commercial salad dressings and mayonnaise
- some spice mixtures
- mustard
- some marinades
- soy sauce
- frozen chips
- teriyaki sauce
- pretzels
- Bombay mix
- scotch eggs
- white pepper
- commercial bouillon
- powdered gravy and sauce mixes
- frozen meals
- hamburgers
- sausages
- processed meat
- hot dogs
- drinking chocolate
- malted milk drinks
- beer, lager, stout or ale
- some fizzy drinks
- natural supplements and vitamins
- body lotions and creams
- toothpastes
- medicines
- make-up and lipsticks
- commercial play-dough mixes.

Cross-contamination

Cross-contamination can occur very easily in the kitchen. Toasters, grills, pans, chopping boards, utensils, appliances and oils that were used for preparing or cooking foods containing gluten may still have traces of gluten in them which can contaminate your gluten-free food. It is essential that a strict cleaning regime is adhered to in order to eliminate the risk of cross-contamination. Cooking oil which has been used to deep-fry foods containing gluten or coated with a gluten containing product such as breadcrumbs, should never be reused to fry gluten-free food. Care should also be taken when baking with ordinary flour as residues of flour can remain in the air for up to 24 hours and settle on counters and gluten-free food such as fresh fruit. It is also important to be vigilant for crumbs in foods like butter which can be passed from knives used for spreading on non gluten-free bread. Gluten-free foods should be stored separately in the kitchen, separate chopping boards should be used and a separate toaster should be used to make gluten-free toast. Gluten can also be found in medicines, vitamins and supplements, lipstick, make-up, toothpaste, body lotions and creams so it is important to bear this in mind when using these products and to ask for gluten-free alternatives. It can also be found in play-dough mixes so this needs to be kept in mind when young children are playing with it.

Hidden Gluten When Eating Out

Some restaurants today offer gluten-free items on their menus and, if not, many good chefs are now willing to provide a gluten-free alternative on request. However, this is not always the case and catering professionals need to be better informed with regards to gluten-free products and cooking. Hidden gluten is in many prepared and processed foods such as sauces and gravy. Therefore, when eating out it is essential that you do not eat anything that is cooked with sauces, dressings or creams unless it is stated as being gluten-free on the menu. If in any doubt, the best way to reduce the risk is to keep your food as plain as possible and to ask for any creams, dressings or sauces to be removed from the meal. It is also better to ask for the meat, poultry or fish to be boiled, steamed or cooked in

olive oil to prevent cross-contamination. If gluten-free pasta or noodles are being served, ensure that they are cooked in clean water that has not been used to cook normal pasta. Chips are a common source of cross-contamination and hidden gluten as they are cooked in oil that has been used to fry non gluten-free foods and gluten is also often added in the manufacturing process. Be cautious also when ordering desserts, ice creams, frozen yogurts and custards as they may contain gluten.

Gluten-free Alternatives

Wheat flour performs a range of functions such as thickening, binding, changing texture, absorbing moisture and adding flavour to the product. There is no single alternative to wheat flour that can replicate all these functions. Therefore, it is commonly suggested that you mix or use a combination of several flours or starches when making a substitute for wheat flour. Different flour mixtures are suggested depending upon the recipe. There is no one ideal mixture for all recipes and it is often necessary to experiment and customize the flour mix to suit the recipe. A wide variety of gluten-free flours, starches and baking aids can be used to produce high quality food, although it is often a case of trial and error when baking gluten-free products.

Baking without gluten can be a challenge as gluten provides important properties to various types of baked products like cakes, pastries, breads, biscuits and cookies. Gluten is the substance which adds the texture to baking products and it is needed for its gas-retaining ability so that a lighter consistency is produced. Gluten-free bread is possibly the most difficult product to bake but with experimentation it can be achieved.

Eggs are the most common binder in gluten-free baking as they replace many of the functions of gluten. Binding can also be assisted by adding cream cheese to a sweet pastry or cheese for savoury. Other additives can be used to replace the gas which is lost when gluten-free flours are used instead of wheat flours.

The most popular additive today is xanthan gum which, used in small quantities, can imitate the spring in bread, bind pastry and prevent biscuits or cookies from becoming too crumbly. Xanthan gum can be bought in supermarkets, health food shops and online. As there is no gluten to develop in gluten-free flours, kneading time will be greatly reduced during preparation. Lost moisture is also a major factor in gluten-free baking; however, this can be improved by using products such as glycerine, oil, honey or syrup or adding natural yogurt or buttermilk to the recipe. Chocolate, fruit, spices, vanilla and nuts are all excellent ingredients for adding flavour and improving texture.

It is important to cover and store gluten-free baked products properly as they quickly lose moisture. It is best to store them in the refrigerator, in an airtight container or in the freezer (if suitable) to prevent this from happening. Gluten-free baked products can be warmed for a short time in the oven or for a few moments in the microwave prior to eating to improve the texture.

Ready Mixed Gluten-free Flour

Fortunately, ready mixed gluten-free plain, self-raising and bread flour is now available to buy. Ready mixed gluten-free plain flour is best used for biscuits, cookies and pastry. Ready mixed gluten-free self-raising flour is best used for cakes and certain breads. Ready mixed bread flour is used primarily for breads but is suitable for some pastries. They have been tried and tested to give excellent results and are often a good starting ground for gluten-free baking. However, there are many different types of flours which are gluten-free and when combined can make an excellent substitute for wheat flour in baking. These can all be bought in supermarkets, health food shops and online.

Gluten-free Flours and Starches

Amaranth

Amaranth flour is made from the seed of the amaranth plant. It has a pleasant peppery flavour and helps to add nutritional value, improve structure and provide binding. It is best used in conjunction with other gluten-free flours.

Arrowroot

Arrowroot flour is ground from the root of the arrowroot plant. It is similar to cornflour and it is used as a thickener in baking and sauces.

Brown Rice Flour

Brown rice flour is heavier and more nutritious than white rice flour. It has a nutty taste and it can add texture. It is best used in conjunction with other gluten-free flours.

Buckwheat

Buckwheat, despite the name, does not contain wheat. It has a strong, bitter flavour and is ideal for pancakes or yeast breads in conjunction with other gluten-free flours.

Chia

Chia flour is made from ground chia seeds. It is highly nutritious and has become very popular in recent years. It is best used in conjunction with other gluten-free flours.

Cornflour

This is made from very finely ground corn. It is quite bland in flavour but it is an excellent thickener that is often used in baking. It is sometimes referred to as corn starch.

Flaxseed

This has a nutty, strong flavour and it also adds colour. It retains moisture and helps to provide a spring to baked goods.

Gram Flour

This is made from ground chickpeas. It is often used in Indian cookery for various types of breads, such as poppadoms and flatbreads.

Hemp

Hemp flour has a nutty flavour and is best used in conjunction with other gluten-free flours.

Millet

This has a powdery texture and is similar in colour to polenta. It has a sweet flavour and is often used in muffins and flatbreads.

Nut Flours (including Almond, Chestnut, Hazelnut, Pecan and Walnut)
Nut flours are used in conjunction with other gluten-free flours. They add flavour, texture and nutritional value to baked goods.

Polenta/Corn Meal

This can be added to baked goods to provide colour, increase moisture and improve flavour. It is often used for muffins and bread.

Potato Flour

This should not be confused with potato starch. Potato flour has a strong flavour and is very heavy so it should be used sparingly in recipes.

Potato Starch

This is weak in flavour but it helps to retain moisture and provides a soft light texture to baked goods.

Quinoa

This has a slightly mild nutty flavour. It is an excellent source of nutrition and is suitable for cakes, biscuits, cookies and breads.

Sorghum

This has a nutty, sweet flavour and is best used in conjunction with other gluten-free flours.

Soya

Soya flour is best used in conjunction with other gluten-free flours. It is used as a thickener or for its nutty taste.

Teff

This is a grain native to North Africa. It tastes very similar to hazelnuts and it is often used to add nutritional value to baked goods.

Tapioca Flour

This has a sweet flavour and is used to add texture and colour in baked goods. It is best used in conjunction with other gluten-free flours.

White Rice Flour

This is neutral in flavour and is not as nutritious as brown rice flour. It can be used alone or in conjunction with other gluten-free flours.

Gluten-free Flour Mixes

For the purpose of convenience, the majority of the recipes in this book have been developed using commercially made, ready mixed plain or self-raising flour. It is important that only the stated flour is used when trying the recipe at home as the wrong one will affect the final outcome of the baked product.

Although it is convenient to have commercially made, ready mixed gluten-free flour at home, it may be more economical to make your own gluten-free flour mixes. These mixes can be made in bulk by doubling or tripling a recipe and stored or frozen until required. Making your own mixes also gives the advantage of being able to customize them to suit your own palate.

There are a number of homemade flour mixes which can be achieved by combining a mixture of different gluten-free flours and starches. It is important to bear in mind that because gluten-free flour does not behave in the same way as wheat flour, a gluten-free mix may work well for one recipe but may not suit another.

Gluten-free All Purpose Flour Mix

250 g/9 oz sorghum flour or brown rice flour

250 g/9 oz tapioca flour

100 g/3½ oz almond flour

1 tsp xanthan gum

Gluten-free Self-Raising Flour Mix

To make self-raising flour simply add 1½ tsp of gluten-free baking

powder per 250 g/9 oz of the gluten-free all purpose flour mix

Gluten-free Cake Flour Mix

250 g/9 oz brown rice flour

250 g/9 oz sorghum flour

250 g/9 oz tapioca flour

Gluten-free Bread Flour Mix

200 g/7 oz soya flour

100 g/3½ oz tapioca flour

200 g/7 oz potato flour

150 g/5½ cornflour

1 tsp xanthan gum

Chapter 1
Cupcakes, Muffins & Small Cakes

raspberry & white chocolate cupcakes

Prep Time: 20 minutes   Cook Time: 18–20 minutes
Per cupcake: 371 kcals/19g fat/7g saturated fat/50g carbs/37g sugar/0.4g salt

makes 12

2 eggs

175 g/6 oz caster sugar

1 tsp glycerine

150 g/5½ oz gluten-free, wheat-free self-raising flour

15 g/½ oz rice flour

½ tsp xanthan gum

1 tsp gluten-free baking powder

20 g/¾ oz ground almonds

35 g/1¼ oz gluten-free white chocolate drops

125 ml/4 fl oz sunflower oil

50 ml/2 fl oz milk

50 ml/2 fl oz single cream

½ tsp vanilla extract

25–30 fresh or frozen raspberries

frosting (optional)

225 g/8 oz icing sugar

60 g/2¼ oz butter, softened

70 g/2½ oz cream cheese

1 tbsp milk or single cream

fresh raspberries, to decorate

1. Preheat the oven to 180°C/350°F/Gas 4. Line a 12-hole muffin tray with paper muffin cases.

2. Whisk the eggs, sugar and glycerine in a large bowl until thick and fluffy. Sift the flours, xanthan gum, baking powder and ground almonds into a separate bowl.

3. Add the dry mixture to the wet mixture and fold in the chocolate drops. Add the oil, milk, cream and vanilla extract and whisk together to form a smooth batter.

4. Divide the mixture between the muffin cases then press 2 raspberries into the centre of each cupcake.

5. Bake the cupcakes in the preheated oven for 18–20 minutes until well-risen and golden. Remove from the oven and cool on a wire rack.

6. To make the frosting, whisk all the ingredients together in a large bowl until thick. Place in a piping bag and decorate each cupcake when completely cool.

chocolate & macadamia nut cupcakes

Prep Time: 25 minutes   Cook Time: 25–30 minutes
Per cupcake: 317 kcals/21g fat/10g saturated fat/30g carbs/17g sugar/0.6g salt

makes 12

200 g/7 oz caster sugar

½ tsp glycerine

190 g/6½ oz butter, softened

4 eggs, beaten

55 g/2 oz gluten-free cocoa powder

175 g/6 oz gluten-free, wheat-free self-raising flour

¼ tsp gluten-free baking powder

¼ tsp xanthan gum

70 g/2½ oz macadamia nuts, chopped

1. Preheat the oven to 180°C/350°F/Gas 4. Line a 12-hole large muffin tray with deep paper cases.

2. Cream the sugar, glycerine and butter together in a large bowl. Mix in the eggs slowly, one at a time.

3. Sift the cocoa powder, flour, baking powder and xanthan gum into the creamed mixture and mix gently together. Carefully fold in half of the macadamia nuts with 45ml/ 3 tbsp warm water.

4. Divide the mixture between the paper cases and sprinkle with the remaining nuts.

5. Bake in the preheated oven for 25-30 minutes or until the nuts are golden and the sponges spring back when lightly touched in the middle. Remove the cupcakes from the oven and cool on a wire rack.

carrot cupcakes with almond & lime frosting

Prep Time: 20 minutes   Cook Time: 18–20 minutes
Per cupcake: 400 kcals/21g fat/7g saturated fat/54g carbs/42g sugar/0.4g salt

makes 9

115 g/4 oz light soft brown sugar

90 ml/6 tbsp sunflower oil

2 eggs

a pinch of saffron strands, crumbled

115 g/4 oz gluten-free, wheat-free self-raising flour, sifted

½ tsp gluten-free baking powder

1 tsp xanthan gum

½ tsp mixed spice

235 g/8½ oz grated carrot

50 g/1¾ oz chopped walnuts

frosting

100 g/3½ oz cream cheese

40 g/1½ oz butter, softened

10 g/¼ oz ground almonds

zest of 2 limes

250 g/9 oz icing sugar

25 g/1 oz flaked almonds, to decorate

1. Preheat the oven to 180°C/350°F/Gas 4. Line 9 holes of a 12-hole deep muffin tray with paper cases.

2. Beat together the sugar, oil, eggs and saffron in a large bowl until creamy. Then add the sifted flour, baking powder, xanthan gum, mixed spice, grated carrot and chopped walnuts and mix gently together.

3. Divide the mixture between the paper cases and bake the cupcakes in the preheated oven for 18–20 minutes until well-risen and golden. Remove from the oven and cool on a wire rack.

4. To make the frosting, process the cream cheese, butter, ground almonds, lime zest and icing sugar until fluffy in a food processor.

5. Place the frosting in a piping bag and decorate each cupcake with swirls of frosting when completely cool. Finish by sprinkling over the flaked almonds.

banana muffins with maple cream frosting

Prep Time: 20 minutes   Cook Time: 25–30 minutes
Per muffin: 480 kcals/20g fat/12g saturated fat/75g carbs/56g sugar/0.7g salt

makes 12

120 g/4¼ oz butter

160 g/5¾ oz soft brown sugar

2 eggs

125 ml/4 fl oz single cream

2 tbsp maple syrup

1 tbsp glycerine

225 g/8 oz gluten-free self-raising flour, sifted

½ tsp gluten-free bicarbonate of soda

425 g/15 oz banana, mashed

frosting

55 g/2 oz butter, softened

125 g/4½ oz cream cheese

375 g/13 oz icing sugar

4 tbsp maple syrup, plus extra to serve (optional)

1. Preheat the oven to 180°C/350°F/Gas 4. Line a 12-hole muffin tray with paper muffin cases.

2. In a food processor, process the butter and soft brown sugar until fluffy. Add the eggs and then slowly mix in the cream, maple syrup, glycerine, sifted flour and bicarbonate of soda. Fold in the mashed bananas.

3. Divide the mixture between the paper cases and bake the muffins in the preheated oven for 25–30 minutes until well-risen and golden. Remove from the oven and place on a wire rack to cool.

4. To make the frosting, process the butter, cream cheese, icing sugar and maple syrup until fluffy in a food processor.

5. Place the frosting in a piping bag and pipe the frosting onto each muffin when completely cool. Serve with maple syrup if using.

fudge frosted chocolate muffins

Prep Time: 20 minutes   Cook Time: 15–20 minutes
Per muffin: 558 kcals/28g fat/16g saturated fat/76g carbs/61g sugar/0.7g salt

makes 12

50 g/1¾ oz gluten-free dark chocolate, broken into pieces

175 g/6 oz butter

175 g/6 oz caster sugar

3 eggs

½ tsp vanilla essence

½ tsp glycerine

175 g/6 oz gluten-free, wheat-free self-raising flour

½ tsp gluten-free baking powder

1 tsp xanthan gum

40 g/1½ oz ground almonds

frosting

90 g/3¼ oz gluten-free dark chocolate, broken into pieces

120 g/4¼ oz butter

450 g/1 lb icing sugar

185 ml/6½ fl oz milk

½ tsp vanilla essence

1. Preheat the oven to 180°C/350°F/Gas 4. Line a 12-hole muffin tray with paper muffin cases.

2. Melt the chocolate in a heatproof bowl set over a pan of simmering water. In a separate bowl, beat the butter and caster sugar together, then mix in the eggs, one at a time, and add the vanilla essence and glycerine. Once the chocolate has cooled slightly, add it to the butter and egg mixture.

3. Sift the flour, baking powder and xanthan gum into a bowl and add the ground almonds. Then stir the dry mixture gently into the chocolate and egg mixture.

4. Spoon the mixture into the muffin cases and bake the muffins in the preheated oven for 15–20 minutes or until a skewer comes out clean when inserted. Remove from the oven and cool on a wire rack.

5. To make the frosting, melt the chocolate and butter in a heatproof bowl set over a pan of simmering water. Mix the icing sugar, half the milk and vanilla essence in a separate bowl and slowly add the chocolate mixture. Add the rest of the milk to get the desired consistency.

6. Place the frosting in a piping bag and decorate each muffin when completely cool.

blueberry & oatmeal muffins

Prep Time: 15 minutes   Cook Time: 20–25 minutes
Per muffin: 260 kcals/11.5g fat/1.5g saturated fat/38g carbs/15g sugar/0.4g salt

makes 9

250 ml/9 fl oz pure orange juice

60 g/2¼ oz gluten-free, wheat-free porridge oats

100 g/3½ oz caster sugar

200 g/7 oz gluten-free, wheat-free plain flour, sifted

½ tsp xanthan gum

1½ tsp gluten-free baking powder

½ tsp gluten-free bicarbonate of soda

½ tsp cinnamon

¼ tsp mixed spice

125 ml/4 fl oz vegetable oil

1 egg, beaten

1 tsp glycerine

175 g/6 oz blueberries

demerara sugar, to sprinkle

1. Preheat the oven to 180°C/350°F/Gas 4. Line a 9-hole deep muffin tray with paper muffin cases.

2. Add the orange juice to the porridge oats and mix well in a bowl.

3. In a separate bowl, mix the sugar, flour, xanthan gum, baking powder, bicarbonate of soda and spices. Add the oil, egg and glycerine to the dry mixture and mix well. Then add the oat mixture and blueberries and fold these in gently.

4. Divide the mixture between the muffin cases and sprinkle with demerara sugar.

5. Bake the muffins in the preheated oven for 20–25 minutes or until a skewer comes out clean when inserted. Remove from the oven and cool on a wire rack.

honey & lemon corn muffins

Prep Time: 15 minutes   Cook Time: 18–20 minutes
Per muffin: 159 kcals/5.5g fat/1g saturated fat/25g carbs/8.5g sugar/0.25g salt

makes 12

125 g/4½ oz gluten-free, wheat-free plain flour

120 g/4¼ oz gluten-free, wheat-free cornmeal

55 g/2 oz caster sugar

2 tsp gluten-free baking powder

¼ tsp xanthan gum

1 egg

juice and zest of ½ lemon

50 ml/2 fl oz vegetable oil

225 ml/8 fl oz milk

2 tbsp honey

1 tbsp glycerine

1. Preheat the oven to 180°C/350°F/Gas 4. Line a 12-hole muffin tray with paper muffin cases.

2. Place the flour, cornmeal, sugar, baking powder and xanthan gum into a bowl and mix together well.

3. In a separate bowl, mix together all the remaining liquid ingredients. Add the liquid mixture to the dry mixture and fold in gently.

4. Spoon the mixture into the muffin cases and bake the muffins in the preheated oven for 18–20 minutes until well-risen and golden. Remove from the oven and cool on a wire rack.

apple & cinnamon bran muffins

Prep Time: 15 minutes   Cook Time: 20–25 minutes
Per muffin: 300 kcals/8g fat/1.5g saturated fat/52g carbs/29g sugar/0.3g salt

makes 12

4 tbsp vegetable oil

1 tbsp glycerine

175 g/6 oz apple purée

2 eggs

½ tsp vanilla essence

55 g/2 oz runny honey

75 ml/2½ fl oz milk

300 g/10½ oz gluten-free,
wheat-free plain flour

120 g/4¼ oz gluten-free,
wheat-free oat bran

70 g/2½ oz ground flax seed

1 tsp gluten-free baking
powder

½ tsp gluten-free
bicarbonate of soda

½ tsp xanthan gum

1 tsp cinnamon

¼ tsp mixed spice

175 g/6 oz soft brown sugar

125 g/4½ oz raisins and
sultanas

1. Preheat the oven to 180°C/350°F/Gas Mark 4. Line a 12-hole muffin tray with paper muffin cases.

2. In a large bowl, whisk together the vegetable oil, glycerine, apple purée, eggs, vanilla essence, honey and milk. In a separate bowl, mix all the dry ingredients together then add the liquid mixture and stir well.

3. Divide the mixture between the paper cases. Bake the muffins in the preheated oven for 20–25 minutes or until a skewer comes out clean when inserted. Remove from the oven and cool on a wire rack.

chocolate & vanilla whoopie pies

Prep Time: 15 minutes   Cook Time: 15–20 minutes
Per pie: 350 kcals/22g fat/13g saturated fat/37g carbs/26g sugar/0.7g salt

makes 10

125 g/4½ oz butter,
plus extra for greasing

115 g/4 oz soft brown sugar

2 eggs

2 tsp vanilla essence

1 tsp glycerine

115 g/4 oz gluten-free,
wheat-free plain flour

1 tsp gluten-free baking
powder

½ tsp gluten-free
bicarbonate of soda

1 tsp xanthan gum

30 g/1 oz gluten-free
cocoa powder

160 ml/5½ fl oz milk

buttercream

85 g/3 oz butter, softened

140 g/5 oz icing sugar, plus
extra for sprinkling

2 tbsp double cream

1. Preheat the oven to 200°C/400°F/Gas Mark 6. Grease two large baking trays and line with baking or silicone paper.

2. Cream the butter, sugar, eggs, vanilla essence and glycerine in a bowl. Sift all the dry ingredients into the bowl and fold into the batter. Slowly add just enough milk to make a smooth mixture.

3. Use two teaspoons to shape 20 walnut-sized balls of the mixture and place them well apart on the prepared baking trays.

4. Bake in the preheated oven, one tray at a time, for 8–10 minutes, or until just risen and firm to the touch. Cool on a wire rack.

5. To make the buttercream, whip the butter, icing sugar and cream together until creamy.

6. To assemble, spread or pipe the buttercream filling on the flat side of half of the cakes. Top with the rest of the cakes. Arrange on a serving plate and sift over icing sugar.

rocky road cake pops

Prep Time: 15 minutes, plus chilling time   Cook Time: No cooking
Per pop: 287 kcals/18g fat/9g saturated fat/31g carbs/25g sugar/0.3g salt

makes 40

1 chocolate brownie cake
(hazelnuts and white
chocolate optional -
see recipe on page 64)

1½ tbsp single cream

250 g/9 oz icing sugar

4 tbsp butter, softened

225 g/8 oz cream cheese

350 g/12 oz gluten-free dark
chocolate, broken into
pieces

toppings

1 bowl of mini
marshmallows

1 bowl of chopped walnuts

1 bowl of gluten-free
digestive biscuit crumbs

1. Make the brownie cake as per recipe on page 64 and allow to cool. Crumble the cake into a large bowl using your fingertips.

2. Mix the cream, icing sugar, butter and cream cheese until smooth and creamy. Add the brownie mixture and stir with a spatula.

3. Knead the mix with your hands to form a dough (if the mix is too dry add a little more cream). Refrigerate until the mixture is firm to the touch.

4. Line 1–2 baking trays with baking paper. Roll out 2.5–5-cm/1–2-inch cake balls from the dough and place on the baking trays. Insert a lollypop stick into each ball. Put the baking trays into the freezer for 30 minutes.

5. Melt the chocolate in a heatproof bowl set over a pan of simmering water, stirring well as it melts. When the cake balls have hardened, remove them from the freezer and dip and cover each one with the melted chocolate. Sprinkle on the marshmallows, chopped walnuts and biscuit crumbs. Return to the baking trays to set.

vanilla, cinnamon & chocolate doughnuts

Prep Time: 1 hour plus rising   Cook Time: 20–25 minutes
Per doughnut: 190 kcals/10g fat/3g saturated fat/22g carbs/10g sugar/1.8g salt

makes 24

yeast mix

125 ml/4 fl oz tepid water

10 g/¼ oz dried yeast

1½ tsp honey

doughnuts

300 g/10½ oz gluten-free, wheat-free self-raising flour

60 g/2¼ oz brown rice flour

¼ tsp xanthan gum

¼ tsp gluten-free baking powder

¼ tsp ground nutmeg

¼ tsp ground cinnamon

60 g/2¼ oz butter, softened

100 g/3½ oz ground almonds

½ tsp vanilla essence

1 egg plus 1 egg yolk

1 tbsp buttermilk

24 gluten-free dark chocolate buttons

vegetable oil, for greasing and frying

150 g/5½ oz caster sugar, to dust

20 g/¾ oz ground cinnamon, to dust

chocolate sauce, to serve

vanilla ice cream, to serve

1. To make the yeast mix, add the tepid water to the dried yeast in a jug and stir in the honey. Leave to stand at room temperature for 15 minutes until frothy.

2. Sift the flours, xanthan gum, baking powder, nutmeg and cinnamon into a large bowl. Rub the butter into the flour mixture using your fingertips, until the mixture resembles fine breadcrumbs. Stir in the almonds, vanilla essence, egg, egg yolk and buttermilk. Pour in the yeast mix and stir well to form a dough, adding a little more water if required. Leave in a warm place until doubled in size.

3. Form 24 small dough balls and insert a chocolate button inside each one. Place them onto a baking tray covered in greased baking paper and cover with greased clingfilm for 40 minutes.

4. Make the sugar dusting for the doughnuts by mixing the caster sugar and ground cinnamon together.

5. Heat enough oil to just cover the doughnuts in a large pan or deep-fryer to 180°–190°C/350°–375°F, or until a cube of bread browns in 30 seconds. Cook the doughnuts in the hot oil (3–4 at a time) for 2–3 minutes on each side until golden brown.

6. Drain on kitchen paper and roll in the sugar dusting. Serve with chocolate sauce and vanilla ice cream.

1

3

6

Chapter 2
Biscuits & Bars

apricot & coconut bars

Prep Time: 25 minutes   Cook Time: 10 minutes plus chilling
Per bar: 252 kcals/15g fat/8.5g saturated fat/28g carbs/17g sugar/0.5g salt

makes 24

450 g/1 lb gluten-free
digestive biscuits

260 g/9¼ oz dried apricots

20 g/¾ oz sesame seeds

250 g/9 oz butter,
plus extra for greasing

2 tbsp honey

400 ml/14 fl oz can
condensed milk

30 g/1 oz desiccated coconut

10 g/¼ oz flaked almonds

1. Grease a 25- x 18-cm/10- x 7-inch rectangular baking tray and line it with baking paper.

2. In a food processor blitz the biscuits on pulse until they are crushed. Set aside. Add the apricots to the processor and blitz until finely chopped.

3. Place the apricots and biscuits in a large bowl and add the sesame seeds.

4. Place the butter, honey and condensed milk in a heavy pan, cook over a low heat, stirring until the mixture is smooth and melted. Continue to cook over a low heat, stirring for 3–4 minutes or until the mixture has thickened slightly. Remove from the heat, cool slightly and then add the crushed biscuits, apricots and sesame seeds.

5. Place the mixture on the baking tray and smooth out with a palette knife to fit the tray. Sprinkle with the coconut and flaked almonds and refrigerate for 2–3 hours until set.

6. When set, cut into bars. The bars can be stored in an airtight container for up to one week.

3

4

5

chewy chocolate & mixed berry bars

Prep Time: 30 minutes   Cook Time: 30 minutes
Per bar: 207 kcals/7g fat/4g saturated fat/32g carbs/24g sugar/0.3g salt

makes 16

225 g/8 oz soft brown sugar

125 g/4½ oz butter,
plus extra for greasing

2 eggs, beaten

115 g/4 oz gluten-free,
wheat-free plain flour

¼ tsp xanthan gum

1 tsp gluten-free baking
powder

3 tbsp gluten-free cocoa
powder

50 g/1¾ oz desiccated
coconut

100 g/3½ oz mixed dried
berries

fudge topping

3 tbsp gluten-free cocoa
powder

160 g/5¾ oz icing sugar

½ tsp vanilla essence

15 g/½ oz butter, melted

2 tbsp warm water

1. Preheat the oven to 180°C/350°F/Gas Mark 4. Grease a 20- x 30-cm/8- x 12-inch baking tray and line with baking paper.

2. Cream the sugar and butter together in a large bowl until pale and fluffy. Add the eggs gradually, one at a time, mixing well after each addition. Sift the flour, xanthan gum, baking powder and cocoa into the egg mixture and fold in gently. Add the coconut and the berries and mix well.

3. Spoon the mixture into the baking tray and smooth with a spatula or palette knife.

4. Bake in the preheated oven for 30 minutes until well-risen. Remove from the oven and cool on a wire rack.

5. To make the fudge topping, sift the cocoa powder and icing sugar into a bowl. Add the vanilla essence, melted butter and warm water and mix until the mixture is easy to spread.

6. Spread on top of the baked cake when cooled completely and refrigerate. When set, cut into bars. The bars can be stored in an airtight container for up to 2 weeks.

breakfast cereal bars

Prep Time: 10 minutes   Cook Time: 30–35 minutes
Per bar: 240kcals/14g fat/7g saturated fat/22g carbs/12g sugar/0.3g salt

makes 12

100 g/3½ oz butter, softened, plus extra for greasing

30 g/1 oz light muscovado sugar

2 tbsp golden syrup

2 eggs, beaten

100 g/3½ oz millet flakes

70 g/2½ oz raisins

55 g/2 oz quinoa

50 g/1¾ oz dried cranberries

70 g/2½ oz sultanas

25 g/1 oz pumpkin seeds

25 g/1 oz sesame seeds

25 g/1 oz chopped walnuts

35 g/1¼ oz desiccated coconut

1. Preheat the oven to 180°C/350°F/Gas Mark 4. Grease a 25- x 18-cm/10- x 7-inch baking tray and line it with baking paper.

2. Beat together the butter, sugar and syrup until creamy in a large bowl. Add all the remaining ingredients and stir well until combined.

3. Place the mixture in the tin and level the surface with a spatula or palette knife.

4. Bake in the preheated oven for 30–35 mins or until golden brown.

5. When cool, turn out onto a flat surface and cut into 12 bars. The bars can be stored in an airtight container for up to 1 week.

rocky road snack bars

Prep Time: 10 minutes   Cook Time: 10 minutes plus chilling
Per bar: 290 kcals/19g fat/12g saturated fat/30g carbs/22g sugar/0.3g salt

makes 16

125 g/4½ oz butter, plus extra for greasing

35 g/1¼ oz golden syrup

250 g/9 oz gluten-free dark chocolate, broken into pieces

150 g/5½ oz gluten-free, wheat-free digestive biscuits or cookies

75 g/2¾ oz mini marshmallows

30 g/1 oz chopped brazil nuts

160 g/5¾ oz sultanas

115 g/4 oz desiccated coconut

1. Grease a 25- x 18-cm/10- x 7-inch baking tray and line it with baking paper.

2. Put the butter, syrup and chocolate in a heatproof bowl set over a pan of simmering water, making sure that the bowl does not touch the water. Melt until glossy and smooth in texture.

3. In a separate bowl, break the biscuits into small pieces and add the remaining dry ingredients. Pour in the chocolate mixture and stir well until combined.

4. Tip the chocolate mixture into the prepared tin and smooth the surface. Chill in the refrigerator for 2–3 hours or until firmly set.

5. When set, cut into bars. The bars can be stored in an airtight container for up to 2 weeks.

roasted hazelnut shortbread

Prep Time: 20 minutes   Cook Time: 10–15 minutes
Per biscuit: 200 kcals/14g fat/8g saturated fat/18g carbs/6g sugar/0.3g salt

makes 18

90 g/3¼ oz icing sugar

190 g/6½ oz gluten-free, wheat-free plain flour, plus extra for dusting

60 g/2¼ oz gluten-free cornflour

35 g/1¼ oz chopped roasted hazelnuts

30 g/1 oz ground almonds

250 g/9 oz butter, plus extra for greasing

½ tsp vanilla essence

caster sugar, for sprinkling

1. Preheat the oven to 180°C/350°F/Gas Mark 4. Grease 1–2 baking trays and line them with baking paper.

2. Put the dry ingredients into a bowl and rub in the butter and vanilla essence until the ingredients form a dough.

3. Turn out onto a floured surface and knead slightly. Roll out to a thickness of 1 cm/½ inch. Cut out 16-18 rounds using a 7-cm/2¾-inch cutter and place on the baking tray.

4. Bake in the preheated oven for 10–15 minutes until golden. Remove from the oven and dust with caster sugar while still warm. Allow to cool on a wire rack.

mandarin & chocolate chip cookies

Prep Time: 15 minutes   Cook Time: 15 minutes
Per cookie: 245 kcals/11g fat/6g saturated fat/35g carbs/15g sugar/0.6g salt

makes 10

120 g/4¼ oz gluten-free dark chocolate

60 g/2¼ oz soft brown sugar

15 g/½ oz caster sugar

70 g/2½ oz butter, plus extra for greasing

1 egg, beaten

250 g/9 oz gluten-free, wheat-free plain flour, plus extra for dusting

½ tsp xanthan gum

1 tbsp gluten-free cocoa powder

1 tsp gluten-free bicarbonate of soda

juice of ½ mandarin orange

zest of 2 mandarin oranges

1. Preheat the oven to 180°C/350°F/Gas Mark 4. Grease a baking tray and line with baking paper.

2. Break or chop the chocolate into small chunks and set aside a quarter of the chunks to top the cookies.

3. Cream the sugars and butter together in a bowl until light and fluffy. Gradually beat in the egg. Add the flour, xanthan gum, cocoa powder, bicarbonate of soda, chocolate chunks, the orange juice and zest.

4. Bring the mixture together by hand into a ball and turn onto a floured surface. Divide into 8–10 rounds, using approximately 2 tablespoons of cookie dough per ball.

5. Place the rounds on a baking tray allowing space in between each cookie for spreading. Flatten each cookie slightly and sprinkle with the reserved chocolate chunks.

6. Bake in the preheated oven for approximately 15 minutes or until just firm to the touch. Remove from the oven and allow to cool on a wire rack.

oatmeal & vanilla cookies

Prep Time: 20 minutes   Cook Time: 18–20 minutes
Per cookie: 192 kcals/9g fat/4.5g saturated fat/28g carbs/14g sugar/0.2g salt

makes 24

135 g/4¾ oz butter, plus extra for greasing

235 g/8½ oz light soft brown sugar

2 eggs, beaten

1 tbsp vanilla essence

175 g/6 oz gluten-free, wheat-free plain flour

1 tsp xanthan gum

1½ tsp gluten-free baking powder

235 g/8½ oz gluten-free rolled oats

175 g/6 oz gluten-free dark chocolate chips

10 g/¼ oz ground almonds

1. Preheat the oven to 180°C/350°F/Gas Mark 4. Grease 1–2 baking trays and line with baking paper.

2. Cream the butter and sugar together in a bowl using a whisk or in a food processor. Slowly add the eggs and vanilla essence, then slowly add the dry ingredients to the bowl and mix until well combined.

3. Divide the mixture into 20–24 balls and place them on the baking trays. Flatten each cookie using wet fingertips and press to shape.

4. Bake in the preheated oven for 18–20 minutes until golden. Remove from the oven and leave to cool on the trays. The cookies can be stored in an airtight container for up to 1 week.

almond & pistachio biscotti

Prep Time: 20 minutes   Cook Time: 35–42 minutes
Per biscotti: 105 kcals/2.5g fat/0.5g saturated fat/17g carbs/8g sugar/trace salt

makes 40

butter, for greasing

2 tsp gluten-free baking powder

245 g/8¾ oz caster sugar

450 g/1 lb gluten-free, wheat-free plain flour

½ tsp xanthan gum

10 g /¼ oz ground almonds

3 large eggs, beaten

60 g/2¼ oz blanched almonds, chopped

60 g/2¼ oz dried cranberries

90 g/3¼ oz dried apricots, chopped

40 g/1½ oz dates, chopped

60 g/2¼ oz pistachio nuts

40 g/1½ oz hazelnuts

1 tsp lime zest

½ tsp vanilla essence

1. Preheat the oven to 180°C/350°F/Gas Mark 4. Grease a baking tray and line it with baking paper.

2. Place the baking powder, sugar, flour, xanthan gum and ground almonds in a large bowl. Add the eggs and mix well. Slowly add the chopped almonds, cranberries, apricots, dates, pistachio nuts, hazelnuts, lime zest and vanilla essence and then mix to form a dough.

3. Roll into 4 cylinder shapes about 5 cm/2 inches in diameter and place on the baking tray, leaving plenty of space in between each one. Slightly press the cylinder shapes down using wet fingertips.

4. Bake in the preheated oven for 18–25 minutes until golden. Remove from the oven and leave to cool. Do not turn the oven off.

5. Diagonally slice each cylinder into 8-10 slices 2.5 cm/ 1 inch thick. Return the slices to the baking tray, cut side down, and bake for a further 7 minutes. Turn the biscotti over and cook the other sides for approximately 10 minutes.

6. Remove from the oven and leave to cool completely on a wire rack.

hazelnut & white chocolate brownies

Prep Time: 25 minutes   Cook Time: 35–40 minutes
Per brownie: 490 kcals/31g fat/15g saturated fat/50g carbs/40g sugar/0.5g salt

makes 12

210 g/7½ oz gluten-free white chocolate, broken into pieces

210 g/7½ oz butter, plus extra for greasing

1 tsp vanilla essence

3 eggs, beaten

300 g/10½ oz caster sugar

115 g/4 oz gluten-free, wheat-free plain flour

1 tsp xanthan gum

1 tsp gluten-free baking powder

30 g/1 oz gluten-free cocoa powder

10 g/¼ oz ground almonds

100 g/3½ oz gluten-free white chocolate chips

100 g/3½ oz chopped roasted hazelnuts

1. Preheat the oven to 160°C/325°F/Gas Mark 3. Grease a 20- x 30-cm/8- x 12-inch baking tin and line with baking paper.

2. Put the white chocolate pieces, butter and vanilla essence in a heatproof bowl set over a pan of simmering water, and heat gently until melted.

3. Let the melted chocolate mixture cool a little. Whisk the eggs and sugar until thick and fluffy then fold into the chocolate mixture. Add the dry ingredients then gently fold in.

4. Spoon the mixture into the baking tin and smooth with a palette knife.

5. Bake in the preheated oven for 30–35 minutes until well-risen and firm to the touch. Remove from the oven and cool in the tin for approximately 1½ hours. Once cool cut into 12 squares.

apricot, cranberry & chocolate chip flapjacks

Prep Time: 15 minutes   Cook Time: 35 minutes
Per flapjack: 192 kcals/10.5g fat/6g saturated fat/22g carbs/11g sugar/0.2g salt

makes 16

115 g/4 oz soft brown sugar

125 g/4½ oz butter, softened, plus extra for greasing

2 tbsp golden syrup

210 g/7½ oz gluten-free, wheat-free porridge oats

40 g/1½ oz cranberries

10 g/¼ oz sunflower seeds

25 g/1 oz desiccated coconut

85 g/3 oz soft dried apricots, roughly chopped

50 g/1¾ oz gluten-free milk chocolate chips

2 tsp mixed spice

1. Preheat the oven to 150°C/300°F/Gas Mark 2. Grease a 25- x 18-cm/10- x 7-inch baking tray and line it with baking paper.

2. Put the sugar, butter and syrup in a saucepan and heat over a medium heat until the sugar has dissolved.

3. Add the rest of the ingredients to a large bowl and pour over the melted butter mixture. Mix well.

4. Put the mixture into the prepared tray and press down until smooth.

5. Bake in the preheated oven for 35 minutes or until golden. Allow to cool in the tray and then cut into pieces. The flapjacks can be stored in an airtight container for up to 1 week (note that the flapjacks are not suitable for freezing).

Chapter 3

Family & Celebration Cakes

carrot cake with lemon cream frosting

Prep Time: 20 minutes   Cook Time: 1 hr 20 minutes
Per cake: 8339 kcals/422g fat/119g saturated fat/1059g carbs/814g sugar/10.4g salt

makes 1 cake

butter, for greasing

250 ml/9 fl oz vegetable oil

290 g/10¼ oz light soft brown sugar

3 eggs

10 g/¼ oz ground almonds

450 g/1 lb carrots, coarsely grated

115 g/4 oz chopped walnuts

375 g/13 oz gluten-free, wheat-free self-raising flour

1 tsp gluten-free bicarbonate of soda

1½ tsp mixed spice

frosting

60 g/2¼ oz butter

160 g/5¾ oz cream cheese

zest of 1 lemon and juice of ½ lemon

500 g/1 lb 2 oz icing sugar, sifted

walnut halves, to decorate (optional)

1. Preheat the oven to 180°C/350°F/Gas Mark 4. Grease a 20-cm/8-inch round cake tin and line with baking paper.

2 . In a large bowl, whisk the oil, sugar and eggs until fluffy, or use a mixer or food processor. Slowly fold in the rest of the ingredients.

3. Pour the mixture into the cake tin and bake on the middle shelf of the preheated oven for 1 hour 20 minutes or until a skewer comes out clean when inserted.

4. Remove from the oven and cool in the tin for approximately 20 minutes. Transfer to a wire rack to cool completely.

5. To make the frosting, using an electric whisk, beat the butter, cream cheese and lemon zest and juice together. Gradually add the sifted icing sugar a little at a time until a smooth frosting forms.

6. Once the cake has cooled, spread the top and sides of the cake with the frosting and decorate with walnuts if desired.

chocolate fudge cake

Prep Time: 20 minutes   Cook Time: 40 minutes
Per cake: 5879 kcals/282g fat/170g saturated fat/776g carbs/642g sugar/7.1g salt

makes 1 cake

125 g/4½ oz gluten-free dark chocolate, broken into pieces

125 g/4½ oz butter, plus extra for greasing

200 g/7 oz light soft brown sugar

100 g/3½ oz caster sugar

1 tsp glycerine

2 eggs, beaten

100 ml/3½ fl oz natural yogurt

½ tsp vanilla essence

100 g/3½ oz rice flour

100 g/3½ oz gluten-free, wheat-free self-raising flour

1 tsp xanthan gum

1½ tsp gluten-free baking powder

½ tsp gluten-free bicarbonate of soda

frosting

150 g/5½ oz gluten-free dark chocolate, broken into pieces

150 ml/5 fl oz double cream

100 g/3½ oz butter

175 g/6 oz icing sugar, sifted

1. Preheat the oven to 180°C/350°F/Gas Mark 4. Grease two 20-cm/8-inch round cake tins and line with baking paper.

2. Melt the chocolate in a heatproof bowl set over a pan of simmering water. In a separate bowl, cream the butter, sugars and glycerine until fluffy and light. Slowly add the eggs, one at a time and beat well. Add the yogurt, vanilla essence and the cooled chocolate mixture. Fold the flours, xanthan gum, baking powder and bicarbonate of soda into the mixture gently. Add a little warm water if the mixture is too stiff.

3. Divide the mixture between the two tins and bake in the preheated oven for 30 minutes or until a skewer comes out clean when inserted.

4. Remove from the oven and allow to cool in the tins for 30 minutes, then transfer to a wire rack to cool completely.

5. To make the frosting, melt the chocolate and cream in a heatproof bowl set over a pan of simmering water. Beat the butter and icing sugar together in a separate bowl and then add the chocolate mixture. Beat well until it reaches a fudge-like consistency.

6. Spread the top of one sponge with some of the fudge frosting and place the other sponge on top. Spread the rest of the fudge frosting over the top and sides of the cake. Refrigerate for 30 minutes. The cake can be stored in an airtight container for 3–4 days.

country-style farmhouse fruit cake

Prep Time: 30 minutes   Cook Time: 1–1¼ hours
Per cake: 2608 kcals/134g fat/69g saturated fat/309g carbs/194g sugar/5.4g salt

makes 1 cake

115 g/4 oz butter, plus extra for greasing

115 g/4 oz light soft brown sugar

2 eggs, beaten

115 g/4 oz gluten-free, wheat-free self-raising flour, sifted

50 g/1¾ oz rice flour

1½ tsp gluten-free baking powder

½ tsp xanthan gum

2 tsp mixed spice

60 g/2¼ oz sultanas

50 g/1¾ oz dried apricots, chopped

1 medium cooking apple, peeled, cored and diced

4 tbsp milk

2 tbsp flaked almonds

1. Preheat the oven to 160°C/325°F/Gas Mark 3. Grease a deep 18-cm/7-inch round loose-based cake tin and line with baking paper.

2. Put the butter and sugar in a bowl and cream together until fluffy. Add the eggs, one at a time, stirring well. Add the flours, baking powder, xanthan gum and mixed spice and mix together gently.

3. Fold in the sultanas, dried apricots, apple and enough of the milk to moisten the mixture.

4. Put the mixture into the cake tin and level with a palette knife. Sprinkle the top with the flaked almonds.

5. Bake in the preheated oven for 1-1¼ hours until golden brown and firm to the touch. Remove from the oven and allow to cool in the tin for 20 minutes, then turn out onto a wire rack. The cake can be served warm or cold.

mocha bundt cake

Prep Time: 20 minutes   Cook Time: 30 minutes
Per cake: 2883 kcals/99g fat/27g saturated fat/429g carbs/254g sugar/6.8g salt

makes 1 cake

2 eggs

3 tbsp instant coffee granules

240 ml/8½ fl oz milk

235 g/8½ oz granulated sugar

60 g/2¼ oz sunflower oil

1 tsp glycerine

1½ tsp vanilla essence

235 g/8½ oz gluten-free, wheat-free plain flour

20 g/¾ oz ground almonds

½ tsp gluten-free baking powder

1 tsp gluten-free bicarbonate of soda

85 g/3 oz gluten-free cocoa powder

½ tsp salt

¾ tsp xanthan gum

butter, for greasing

icing sugar, for dusting

1. Preheat the oven to 180°C/350°F/Gas Mark 4. Lightly grease a 25-cm/10-inch Bundt tin.

2. Whisk together the eggs, coffee, milk, sugar, oil, glycerine and vanilla essence in a large bowl.

3. In a separate bowl, sift together the flour, ground almonds, baking powder, bicarbonate of soda, cocoa powder, salt and xanthan gum. Add the flour mixture to the egg mixture and stir to form a batter.

4. Transfer the batter to the prepared Bundt tin and bake on the middle shelf of the preheated oven for 30 minutes or until a skewer comes out clean when inserted.

5. Remove from the oven and allow to cool in the tin for 45 minutes, then turn out onto a wire rack to cool completely. Dust with icing sugar before serving.

victoria sponge with vanilla cream & strawberries

Prep Time: 20 minutes   Cook Time: 30–35 minutes
Per cake: 6238 kcals/457g fat/246g saturated fat/427g carbs/302g sugar/7.3g salt

makes 1 cake

220 g/7¾ oz butter, plus extra for greasing

220 g/7¾ oz caster sugar

4 eggs, beaten

1 tsp vanilla essence

200 g/7 oz gluten-free, wheat-free plain flour

100 g/3½ oz ground almonds

2 tsp gluten-free baking powder

6 tbsp of gluten-free strawberry jam

1 punnet of strawberries, halved

icing sugar, for dusting

vanilla cream

350 ml/12 fl oz double cream

1 tsp vanilla essence

1. Preheat the oven to 160°C/325°F/Gas Mark 3. Grease two 20-cm/8-inch cake tins and line with baking paper.

2. Cream the butter and sugar in a large bowl. Slowly add the eggs, one at a time, and the vanilla essence, mixing well. Add the flour, ground almonds and baking powder and mix well.

3. Divide the mixture between the two prepared tins and bake in the preheated oven for 30–35 minutes or until the sponge springs back when lightly touched in the centre.

4. Remove from the oven and leave to cool in the tins for approximately 10 minutes. Then turn out onto a wire rack to cool completely.

5. To make the vanilla cream, whip the cream and vanilla essence in a bowl until soft peaks form.

6. When completely cool, sandwich the cakes together with the strawberry jam, vanilla cream and strawberry halves. Dust the top with icing sugar.

chocolate & walnut banana bread

Prep Time: 20 minutes   Cook Time: 40–50 minutes
Per loaf: 4668 kcals/215g fat/104g saturated fat/588g carbs/424g sugar/5.1g salt

makes 1 loaf

20 g/¾ oz rice flour

225 g/8 oz gluten-free, wheat-free plain flour

1 tsp xanthan gum

2 tsp gluten-free baking powder

3 bananas, mashed

235 g/8½ oz caster sugar

125 g/4½ oz butter, melted

2 eggs, beaten

½ tsp vanilla essence

175 g/6 oz gluten-free dark chocolate chips

70 g/2½ oz chopped walnuts

unsalted butter, for greasing and to serve

1. Preheat the oven to 180°C/350°F/Gas Mark 4. Grease a 900-g/2-lb loaf tin and line with baking paper.

2. Sift the flours, xanthan gum and baking powder into a bowl. In a separate bowl, mix the bananas, sugar, butter, eggs, vanilla essence, chocolate chips and walnuts together. Add the flour mix and combine, folding gently.

3. Put the mixture into the prepared loaf tin. Bake in the preheated oven for 40–50 minutes or until golden and risen.

4. Remove from the oven and cool in the tin for 40 minutes before transferring to a wire rack to cool completely. Slice and serve with unsalted butter.

sticky fruit loaf

Prep Time: 15 minutes plus soaking   Cook Time: 1¼–1¾ hours
Per loaf: 5852 kcals/284g fat/133g saturated fat/672g carbs/515g sugar/5.6g salt

makes 1 loaf

350 g/12 oz sultana and raisin mix

zest and juice of 1 lemon

220 g/7¾ oz butter, plus extra for greasing

220 g/7¾ oz dark soft brown sugar

½ tsp glycerine

5 eggs, beaten

250 g/9 oz gluten-free, wheat-free plain flour

2 tsp mixed spice

3 tbsp black treacle

2 tbsp whiskey

60 g/2¼ oz ground almonds

60 g/2¼ oz glacé cherries

60 g/2¼ oz mixed seeds (e.g. sunflower, sesame, millet)

1. Mix the dried fruits with the lemon zest and juice and 60 ml/4 tbsp warm water. Mix well and leave to soak for an hour or until the fruit is plump.

2. Preheat the oven to 150°C/300°F/Gas Mark 2. Grease a 900-g/2-lb loaf tin and line with baking paper.

3. Cream the butter, sugar and glycerine in a large bowl. Add the eggs, one at a time, and stir in. Add the rest of the ingredients, including the dried fruits with their soaking liquid, to the bowl and mix well.

4. Put the mixture into the tin and level it with a palette knife. Bake in the preheated oven for between 1¼ and 1¾ hours or until a skewer comes out clean when inserted.

5. Remove from the oven and cool in the tin for 40 minutes before transferring to a wire rack to cool completely. This loaf improves with age, so make it the day before you want to serve for a really sticky, moist loaf. Store in an airtight container.

banana bread

Prep Time: 20 minutes   Cook Time: 50–60 minutes
Per loaf: 2975 kcals/59g fat/31g saturated fat/516g carbs/278g sugar/6.8g salt

makes 1 loaf

225 g/8 oz soft dark brown sugar

2 eggs, beaten

225 g/8 oz mashed banana

50 g/1¾ oz butter, melted, plus extra for greasing

1 tbsp black treacle

125 ml/4 fl oz buttermilk

375 g/13 oz gluten-free plain flour

1 tsp gluten-free baking powder

1 tsp gluten-free bicarbonate of soda

1 tsp gluten-free mixed spice

unsalted butter, to serve

1. Preheat the oven to 180°C/350°F/Gas Mark 4. Grease a 900-g/2-lb loaf tin and line with baking paper.

2. Put the sugar, eggs, banana, melted butter, treacle and buttermilk in a large bowl and mix well.

3. Sift the flour, baking powder, bicarbonate of soda and mixed spice together. Add to the bowl with the banana mixture and mix until combined.

4. Pour the mixture into the prepared tin and bake in the preheated oven for 50–60 minutes or until golden brown and firm to the touch.

5. Remove from the oven and cool in the tin for 40 minutes before transferring to a wire rack to cool completely. Serve warm or cold, sliced and spread with unsalted butter.

courgette bread

Prep Time: 25 minutes   Cook Time: 55–60 minutes
Per loaf: 2430 kcals/138g fat/18g saturated fat/235g carbs/116g sugar/2.9g salt

makes 2 loaves

butter, for greasing

380 g/13½ oz gluten-free, wheat-free plain flour

1 tsp gluten-free baking powder

2 tsp xanthan gum

1 tsp gluten-free bicarbonate of soda

1 tsp mixed spice

2 tsp cinnamon

225 g/8 oz caster sugar

3 eggs

240 ml/8½ fl oz vegetable oil

2 tsp vanilla essence

115 g/4 oz walnuts, roughly chopped

220 g/7¾ oz courgettes, finely grated

1. Preheat the oven to 160°C/325°F/Gas Mark 3. Grease two 450-g/1-lb loaf tins and line with baking paper.

2. Sift the flour, baking powder, xanthan gum, bicarbonate of soda and spices together into a large bowl.

3. In a separate bowl, whisk the sugar, eggs, vegetable oil and vanilla essence until a creamy consistency forms. Add the flour mixture, walnuts and courgettes to the bowl and fold in to make a smooth batter.

4. Divide the mixture between the two tins and bake in the preheated oven for 55–60 minutes until firm to the touch.

5. Leave to cool in the tins for approximately 20 minutes before transferring to a wire rack to cool. Let the bread rest on the rack for at least 30 minutes before serving.

angel food cake

Prep Time: 15 minutes   Cook Time: 45 minutes
Per cake: 2643 kcals/7g fat/3g saturated fat/579g carbs/407g sugar/3.9g salt

makes 1 cake

butter, for greasing

10 egg whites

60 g/2¼ oz white rice flour

60 g/2¼ oz tapioca flour

60 g/2¼ oz gluten-free cornflour

60 g/2¼ oz potato flour

300 g/10½ oz caster sugar

1½ tsp gluten-free cream of tartar

½ tsp vanilla essence

½ tsp salt

500 g/1 lb 2 oz bag of frozen fruits of the forest (optional)

85 g/3 oz caster sugar (optional)

icing sugar, to decorate

1. Preheat the oven to 180°C/350°F/Gas Mark 4. Grease a 20-cm/8-inch cake tin and line with baking paper.

2. Allow the egg whites to sit for approximately 30 minutes at room temperature in a large bowl. In a separate bowl, sift the white rice flour, tapioca flour, cornflour, potato flour and 175 g/6 oz of the sugar.

3. Using a food processor or mixer, mix the egg whites with the cream of tartar, vanilla essence and salt until soft peaks form. Gradually add the remaining 125 g/4½ oz of sugar until stiff peaks develop. Add the flour mixture and fold in.

4. Spoon the mixture into the prepared tin and bake in the preheated oven for approximately 45 minutes until firm to the touch and a skewer inserted in the centre comes out clean.

5. Remove from the oven and, leaving the cake in the tin, turn upside-down to cool on a wire rack. Poach the fruits of the forest with the caster sugar gently until soft, Allow to cool completely. When the cake is cool, remove from the tin and decorate with icing sugar and the drained mixed fruit, if desired.

black forest gateau

Prep Time: 30 minutes   Cook Time: 25–30 minutes
Per gateau: 8498 kcals/635g fat/345g saturated fat/637g carbs/503g sugar/7.1g salt

makes 1 gateau

200 g/7 oz caster sugar

125 g/4½ oz butter, plus extra for greasing

1 tsp glycerine

90 g/3¼ oz gluten-free dark chocolate, broken into pieces

4 eggs

100 g/3½ oz ground almonds

125 g/4½ oz gluten-free, wheat-free plain flour

4 tbsp gluten-free cornflour

2½ tsp gluten-free baking powder

topping & filling

400 g/14 oz canned black cherries, in syrup

2 tbsp kirsch

6 tbsp black cherry jam

700 ml/1¼ pints double cream, whipped

150 g/5½ oz gluten-free dark chocolate, grated, to decorate

fresh cherries, to decorate

1. Preheat the oven to 180°C/350°F/Gas Mark 4. Grease two 20-cm/8-inch cake tins and line with baking paper.

2. Beat the sugar, butter and glycerine together in a large bowl. Melt the chocolate in a heatproof bowl set over a pan of simmering water and allow to cool slightly. Beat the eggs one at a time into the sugar and butter mixture, adding the almonds with the final egg. Fold in the melted chocolate. Sift in the flour, cornflour and baking powder, and fold together gently.

3. Divide the mixture between the two prepared tins and bake in the preheated oven for 20–25 minutes until firm to the touch.

4. Remove from the oven and cool in the tins for 40 minutes. Drain the cherries reserving 100 ml/3½ fl oz of the syrup. Mix the kirsch with the cherry syrup and pour over the cakes.

5. When the cakes are cool, transfer them to a wire rack. Sandwich the cakes together with the jam, the canned cherries and half the cream. Spread the remaining cream on the top and sides of the cakes and decorate with grated chocolate and fresh cherries.

chocolate & raspberry gateau

Prep Time: 30 minutes   Cook Time: 40 minutes
Per gateau: 6953 kcals/514g fat/315g saturated fat/545g carbs/420g sugar/12.3g salt

makes 1 gateau

90 g/3¼ oz gluten-free cocoa powder, plus extra for dusting

175 g/6 oz butter, plus extra for greasing

240 ml/8½ fl oz full-bodied brewed coffee

200 g/7 oz caster sugar

120 g/4¼ oz gluten-free, wheat-free plain flour

1 tsp gluten-free baking powder

1 tsp gluten-free bicarbonate of soda

¼ tsp xanthan gum

pinch of salt

2 eggs, beaten

125 g/4½ oz full fat yogurt

1 tbsp raspberry liqueur

1 tsp vanilla essence

frosting

175 g/6 oz caster sugar

600 ml/1 pint double cream

2 punnets raspberries, washed, to decorate

1. Preheat the oven to 180°C/350°F/Gas Mark 4. Grease two 23-cm/9-inch springform cake tins and line with baking paper.

2. Put the cocoa powder, butter and the coffee into a pan and simmer on a low heat until the butter has melted. Remove from the heat, mix in the sugar and leave to one side to cool slightly.

3. In a large bowl, mix the flour, baking powder, bicarbonate of soda, xanthan gum and salt together. Add the flour mixture to the cocoa mixture in the pan and stir in until combined. Add the eggs, one at a time, and mix well. Add the yogurt, raspberry liqueur and vanilla essence and stir well.

4. Divide the batter between the prepared tins and bake for 40 minutes or until a skewer comes out clean when inserted.

5. Remove from the oven and allow the cakes to cool in the tins for 20 minutes and then transfer them onto a wire rack to finish cooling.

6. To make the frosting, whip together the sugar and cream in a large bowl. Use half the whipped cream and half the raspberries to sandwich the cakes together and then spread the remaining half of the cream on top of the cake, and decorate with the remaining raspberries.

strawberry shortcakes

Prep Time: 30 minutes   Cook Time: 20–25 minutes
Per shortcake: 482 kcals/26g fat/16g saturated fat/59g carbs/26g sugar/0.5g salt

makes 8

90 g/3¼ oz tapioca flour

115 g/4 oz brown rice flour

1 tbsp gluten-free baking powder

90 g/3¼ oz gluten-free cornflour

½ tsp xanthan gum

¼ tsp gluten-free bicarbonate of soda

10 g/¼ oz ground almonds

70 g/2½ oz butter, plus extra for greasing

125 g/4½ oz caster sugar

175 ml/6 fl oz milk

strawberry filling

650 g/1 lb 7 oz strawberries, hulled

2 tbsp caster sugar

250 ml/9 fl oz double cream

icing sugar, for dusting

1. Preheat the oven to 200°C/400°F/Gas Mark 6. Grease a baking tray and line with baking paper.

2. Sift the tapioca flour, rice flour, baking powder, cornflour, xanthan gum, bicarbonate of soda and ground almonds into a bowl.

3. In a separate bowl, beat the butter and sugar together until it is fluffy. Add the flour mixture and fold in gently. Gradually add enough of the milk to the dry ingredients to form a soft dough.

4. Roll out the dough to a thickness of 2.5 cm/1 inch. Use a 7-cm/2¾-inch fluted round cutter to press out rounds of dough and place well apart on the baking tray. Brush the tops with the remaining milk.

5. Bake in the preheated oven for 20-25 minutes or until risen and golden. Remove from the oven and carefully transfer onto a wire rack to cool.

6. To make the filling, roughly chop the strawberries. Place a third in a blender, add the caster sugar and blitz until smooth. Whip the cream, add half the remaining strawberries and the strawberry coulis and stir gently to swirl the mixture lightly. Split the cooled shortcakes and spread the strawberry cream over the bottom halves. Scatter the remaining chopped strawberries on top. Place on the tops of the shortcakes and dust with icing sugar. Serve immediately.

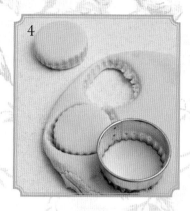

drambuie christmas cake

Prep Time: 40 minutes plus marinating   Cook Time: 2½–3 hours
Per cake: 15567 kcals/433g fat/156g saturated fat/2827g carbs/2462g sugar/7.6g salt

makes 1 cake

85 g/3 oz orange marmalade

100 g/3½ oz dried figs, chopped

100 g/3½ oz dates, chopped

200 g/7 oz raisins

500 g/1 lb 2 oz sultanas

100 g/3½ oz glacé cherries, chopped

200 g/7 oz dried apricots, chopped

160 ml/5½ fl oz Drambuie, plus extra for drizzling

160 g/5¾ oz dark brown soft sugar

250 g/9 oz butter, plus extra for greasing

4 large eggs, beaten

300 g/10½ oz gluten-free, wheat-free plain flour, sifted

1½ tsp mixed spice

100 g/3½ oz blanched almonds, chopped

to decorate

3 tbsp apricot conserve

1 kg/2 lb 4 oz gluten-free ready-to-roll marzipan

icing sugar, for dusting

1 kg/2 lb 4 oz gluten-free ready-to-roll icing

gluten-free silver balls

1. Mix the marmalade, all the fruit and the Drambuie in a bowl, cover with clingfilm and leave to marinate over night.

2. Preheat the oven to 150°C/300°F/Gas Mark 2. Grease a square 20-cm/8-inch cake tin and line with baking paper, extending the paper approximately 5–6 cm/2–2½ inches above the tin.

3. Beat the sugar and butter together in a bowl by hand, or in a food processor, until fluffy. Add the eggs slowly, one at a time. Then add the marinated fruit mixture, the flour, mixed spice and almonds and stir well.

4. Put the mixture in the prepared tin, smooth the surface level and bake in the preheated oven for approximately 2½–3 hours until a skewer inserted into the centre comes out clean.

5. Remove the cake from the tin and leave to cool. Remove the paper from the cake, then use a clean skewer to pierce the surface of the cake and drizzle over Drambuie. Wrap in greaseproof paper and foil and store in a cool place for 3–4 weeks.

6. To decorate, push the conserve through a nylon sieve, then gently heat until runny. Place the cake on a cake board. Brush the conserve over the top and sides of the cake. Roll out half the marzipan on an icing sugar dusted surface and cut out a square large enough for the top of the cake. Roll out the remainder and use to cover the sides of the cake, trimming it to fit. Leave to dry for at least 24 hours.

7. Roll out the icing on an icing sugar dusted surface to a square large enough to cover the top and sides of the cake. Trim the edges, then smooth the surface. Use a star cutter to press into the icing to leave a shape and decorate with silver balls as desired.

lemon zest birthday cake

Prep Time: 25 minutes   Cook Time: 35–40 minutes
Per cake: 4405 kcals/202g fat/117g saturated fat/637g carbs/460g sugar/8.4g salt

makes 1 cake

200 g/7 oz butter, plus extra
for greasing

200 g/7 oz caster sugar

4 eggs, beaten

200 g/7 oz gluten-free,
wheat-free self-raising
flour

2 tsp gluten-free baking
powder

1 tsp xanthan gum

juice and zest of 1 lemon

200 g/7 oz raspberries,
to decorate

lemon icing

250 g/9 oz icing sugar

juice and zest of 1 lemon

1. Preheat the oven to 180°C/350°F/Gas Mark 4. Grease a 20-cm/8-inch round springform cake tin and line with baking paper.

2. Cream the butter and sugar together in a large bowl until fluffy. Slowly add the eggs, one at a time, and stir well. Sift in the flour, baking powder and xanthan gum, then add the lemon juice and lemon zest, and fold into the mixture.

3. Put the mixture into the prepared tin and bake in the preheated oven for 35–40 minutes until a skewer inserted into the centre comes out clean.

4. Remove from the oven and leave to cool in the tin for 45 minutes, before transferring it to a wire rack.

5. To make the icing, mix the icing sugar, lemon juice and lemon zest together in a large bowl. Drizzle the lemon icing over the cake and decorate with the raspberries to serve.

pumpkin & walnut cake

Prep Time: 20 minutes   Cook Time: 40–45 minutes

Per cake: 3639 kcals/240g fat/108g saturated fat/360g carbs/337g sugar/4.3g salt

makes 1 cake

190 g/6½ oz butter, plus extra for greasing

190 g/6½ oz soft light brown sugar

3 eggs, beaten

400 g/14 oz canned pumpkin purée

1 tsp gluten-free bicarbonate of soda

3 tbsp milk

550 g/1 lb 4 oz gluten-free, wheat-free self-raising flour

1 tsp xanthan gum

½ tsp gluten-free baking powder

100 g/3½ oz walnuts, chopped

frosting

150 g/5½ oz icing sugar

pulp and juice of 2 passion fruits

2 tsp lime zest

1. Preheat the oven to 180°C/350°F/Gas Mark 4. Grease a 20-cm/8-inch round, loose-based, deep, cake tin and line with baking paper.

2. Cream the butter and sugar together in a large bowl until fluffy. Stir in the eggs, slowly, one at a time and then stir in the pumpkin.

3. Add the bicarbonate of soda to the milk and then add to the pumpkin mixture.

4. In a separate bowl, sift the flour, xanthan gum and baking powder together and then fold the mixture into the pumpkin mixture with the walnuts.

5. Spoon the mixture into the prepared cake tin and bake in the preheated oven for 40–45 minutes until a skewer inserted into the centre comes out clean.

6. Remove from the oven and then leave to cool in the tin for 10 minutes before transferring to a wire rack to cool completely.

7. To make the frosting, sift the icing sugar into a bowl and then add the passion fruit pulp and juice and the lime zest. Stir well and pour over the cooled cake.

Chapter 4
Desserts & Pies

pear & apple oat crisp

Prep Time: 20 minutes   Cook Time: 30–35 minutes
Per serving: 275 kcals/13g fat/7g saturated fat/34g carbs/27g sugar/2g salt

serves 8

filling

3 apples, peeled, cored and sliced

3 soft pears, peeled, cored and sliced

3 tsp apple juice

½ tsp gluten-free cornflour

½ tsp cinnamon

2 tbsp honey

2 cloves

custard or single cream, to serve

oat crisp

60 g/2¼ oz gluten-free, wheat-free plain flour

100 g/3½ oz light soft brown sugar

20 g/¾ oz walnuts, chopped

60 g/2¼ oz gluten-free porridge oats

100 g/3½ oz butter, plus extra for greasing

1. Preheat the oven to 160°C/325°F/Gas Mark 3. Grease a 23-cm/9-inch pie dish.

2. Put the apple, pear, apple juice, cornflour, cinnamon, honey and cloves in a bowl, and stir well.

3. To make the crisp, mix the flour, sugar, walnuts, oats and butter in a large bowl, rubbing the ingredients together with your fingertips.

4. Spread a small layer of crisp mixture over the base of the pie dish. Arrange the apple and pear mixture on top and sprinkle over the remaining crisp mixture.

5. Bake in the preheated oven for 30–35 minutes until golden brown and crisp on top. Serve with custard or fresh cream.

rhubarb & blackberry crumble

Prep Time: 25 minutes   Cook Time: 50–55 minutes
Per serving: 423 kcals/16.5g fat/9g saturated fat/68g carbs/40g sugar/0.3g salt

serves 6

8–10 sticks of rhubarb, cut into bite-sized pieces (800 g/1 lb 12 oz in weight)

8 tbsp caster sugar

250 g/9 oz blackberries

½ tsp vanilla essence

½ tsp ground ginger

ice cream, double cream or hot custard sauce, to serve

crumble topping

100 g/3½ oz butter, plus extra for greasing

200 g/7 oz gluten-free, wheat-free plain flour

100 g/3½ oz demerara sugar

15 g/½ oz flaked almonds

1. Preheat the oven to 180°C/350°F/Gas Mark 4.

2. Place the rhubarb on a baking tray, sprinkle with the caster sugar and roast in the oven for 12–15 minutes.

3. When cooked, put the rhubarb in a 23-cm/9-inch greased ovenproof dish with the blackberries, vanilla essence and ginger.

4. For the topping, rub the butter and flour together with your fingertips until the mixture resembles fine breadcrumbs. Add the demerara sugar and almonds. Cover the rhubarb with the crumble topping and bake in the preheated oven for 35–40 minutes until golden.

5. Serve with ice cream, double cream or hot custard sauce as preferred.

almond & pear crunch cake

Prep Time: 30 minutes   Cook Time: 55–60 minutes
Per serving: 409 kcals/25g fat/14g saturated fat/44g carbs/22g sugar/0.7g salt

serves 12

175 g/6 oz butter, plus extra for greasing

175 g/6 oz caster sugar

3 large eggs, beaten

½ tsp vanilla essence

175 g/6 oz gluten-free, wheat-free plain flour

2 tsp gluten-free baking powder

½ tsp cinnamon

30 g/1 oz ground almonds

500 g/1 lb 2 oz canned pear halves, drained

whipped cream or custard sauce, to serve

crumble topping

150 g/5½ oz gluten-free, wheat-free plain flour

115 g/4 oz butter

50 g/1¾ oz caster sugar

1 handful of flaked almonds

1. Preheat the oven to 180°C/350°F/Gas Mark 4. Grease a 20-cm/8-inch cake tin and line with baking paper.

2. Cream the butter and sugar together in a bowl until fluffy. Add the eggs slowly, one at a time, mixing well, then add the vanilla essence and stir.

3. Sift in the flour, baking powder and cinnamon, and fold gently into the mixture. Add the ground almonds and fold in.

4. Spoon the mixture into the prepared tin and place the pear halves evenly on top, pushing them down a little.

5. To make the crumble topping, put the flour, butter and sugar into a bowl, and rub together, using your fingertips, to form the crumble. Sprinkle the crumble mixture over the top of the cake and sprinkle with the flaked almonds.

6. Bake on the middle shelf of the preheated oven for 55–60 minutes until golden. Remove from the oven and cool in the tin. Serve with whipped cream or custard sauce.

upside-down banana & maple syrup cake

Prep Time: 30 minutes   Cook Time: 40–45 minutes
Per serving: 236 kcals/13g fat/7g saturated fat/27g carbs/15g sugar/0.4g salt

serves 12

160 g/5¾ oz butter, plus extra for greasing

60 g/2¼ oz brown sugar

4 tbsp maple syrup, plus extra to serve

3–4 bananas, sliced lengthways

235 g/8½ oz caster sugar

4 eggs, beaten

½ tsp vanilla essence

160 g/5¾ oz gluten-free, wheat-free self-raising flour

½ tsp xanthan gum

ice cream, to serve

1. Preheat the oven to 180°C/350°F/Gas Mark 4. Grease a 23-cm/9-inch round springform cake tin. Wrap a piece of foil around the outside of the tin to prevent the syrup from leaking.

2. Heat 60 g/2¼ oz of the butter, brown sugar and maple syrup in a pan until the sugar melts and turns golden. Pour the mixture into the prepared tin and then arrange the sliced bananas cut-side down over the base.

3. Cream the remaining butter and caster sugar together in a bowl until fluffy. Add the eggs, one at a time stirring well, and the vanilla essence. Sift in the flour and xanthan gum and fold gently into the batter.

4. Spoon the mixture over the bananas and smooth with a palette knife.

5. Bake in the preheated oven for 40–45 minutes until golden and the centre springs back when lightly touched. Leave to cool in the tin on a wire rack.

6. Turn out onto a serving plate, and serve with ice cream and maple syrup.

glazed brandy & date bread & butter pudding

Prep Time: 30 minutes plus soaking   Cook Time: 30–35 minutes
Per serving: 866 kcals/51g fat/30g saturated fat/80g carbs/44g sugar/1.3g salt

serves 2

6 dates, diced

3 tbsp brandy

1 tbsp sweet mincemeat

1 tsp caster sugar

butter, for spreading and greasing

4–6 slices gluten-free white bread

2 tsp demerara sugar

custard

125 ml/4 fl oz milk

125 ml/4 fl oz double cream

1 vanilla pod

1 egg

25 g/1 oz caster sugar

1. Soak the dates in the brandy for 6 hours or leave overnight. Then add the mincemeat and caster sugar to the date and brandy mixture.

2. Preheat the oven to 160°C/325°F/Gas Mark 3. Butter two 250-ml/9-fl oz ovenproof dishes.

3. Remove the crusts from the bread, butter the slices and cut into triangles. Fit a layer into the base of each dish. Alternate the date mixture and slices of bread until the dish is full. Finish off with slices of bread, buttered side down, at the top.

4. To make the custard, put the milk, cream and vanilla pod into a pan and bring to the boil. Remove from the heat. In a bowl, whisk the egg and caster sugar together and pour the heated milk mixture into it.

5. Remove the vanilla pod and gradually pour the custard over the bread and butter pudding until it is absorbed. Leave to stand for 15–20 minutes.

6. Place the dishes in a roasting tin, sprinkle over the demerara sugar. Pour boiling water to come half way up the outside of the dishes. Cover the tray loosely with foil and bake for 20 minutes. Remove the foil and bake for a further 5–10 minutes or until the tops are golden. For an extra crunchy top, pop the puddings under a hot grill for a couple of minutes until caramelised. Serve warm or cold.

oven-baked soft-centred chocolate pudding

Prep Time: 15 minutes   Cook Time: 20–25 minutes
Per serving: 686 kcals/43g fat/23g saturated fat/73g carbs/60g sugar/0.7g salt

serves 4

200 g/7 oz gluten-free dark chocolate, broken into pieces

115 g/4 oz unsalted butter, plus extra for greasing

3 tbsp gluten-free, wheat-free plain flour, sifted

3 eggs, beaten

115 g/4 oz caster sugar

3 tbsp ground almonds

1 tsp gluten-free baking powder

½ tsp vanilla essence

½ tsp glycerine

gluten-free cocoa powder, for dusting

vanilla cream or extra thick

1. Preheat the oven to 200°C/400°F/Gas Mark 6.

2. Place the chocolate and butter in a heatproof bowl and set over a pan of simmering water. Stir the mixture until it is just melted and then remove it from the heat.

3. Place the flour, eggs, sugar, almonds, baking powder, vanilla essence and glycerine in a bowl and mix until combined. Slowly stir in the chocolate mixture.

4. Grease four 175-ml/6-fl oz metal dariole moulds. Divide the mixture between the moulds and place on a baking tray. Bake the puddings in the preheated oven for 15–18 minutes.

5. Remove from the oven, gently run a knife around the edge of each pudding and invert onto a serving plate. Dust with cocoa powder and serve immediately with cream.

white chocolate & irish cream cheesecake

Prep Time: 30 minutes   Cook Time: 20 minutes plus chilling
Per serving: 794 kcals/70g fat/42g saturated fat/36g carbs/19g sugar/1g salt

serves 12

biscuit base

350 g/12 oz gluten-free digestive biscuits

150 g/5½ oz butter

filling

5 leaves gelatine

60 g/2¼ oz gluten-free white chocolate drops or buttons

600 g/1 lb 5 oz cream cheese

600 ml/1 pint double cream

100 g/3½ oz caster sugar

100 ml/3½ fl oz Irish cream liqueur

1 tsp vanilla essence

to decorate

25 g/1 oz gluten-free white chocolate drops or buttons

gluten-free drinking chocolate, to dust

1. Crush the biscuits using a food processor or place the biscuits in clingfilm or a polythene bag and crush them with a rolling pin.

2. Melt the butter in a small pan or in a non-metallic bowl on a low heat in the microwave. Add the biscuit crumbs to the melted butter and mix well.

3. Press the crumb mixture into the base of a 20-cm/8-inch round springform cake tin and chill in the refrigerator for approximately 30 minutes.

4. Place the gelatine leaves in a pan of cold water so they can soften.

5. Melt the white chocolate drops in a heatproof bowl set over a pan of simmering water.

6. Put the cream cheese, cream, caster sugar, Irish cream and vanilla essence into a bowl and, using a whisk or electric mixer, whip slowly until thick and creamy. Mix in the melted chocolate.

7. Squeeze the water out of the gelatine leaves and place in a pan over a low heat to melt. Add to the cream cheese mixture and stir in thoroughly and quickly before the gelatine sets.

8. Spoon the cream cheese mixture onto the biscuit base and smooth the top with a palette knife. Refrigerate for 2–3 hours until set.

9. To decorate, melt the white chocolate drops in a heatproof bowl set over a pan of simmering water. Spoon the chocolate into a piping bag with a small nozzle and drizzle it over the top of the cheesecake. Dust the edge with drinking chocolate.

mini cherry pies

Prep Time: 30 minutes plus chilling   Cook Time: 35–40 minutes
Per serving: 380 kcals/10g fat/6g saturated fat/71g carbs/36g sugar/0.6g salt

makes 12

pastry

450 g/1 lb gluten-free, wheat-free self-raising flour, plus extra for dusting

½ tsp xanthan gum

40 g/1½ oz icing sugar

125 g/4½ oz butter, plus extra for greasing

125ml/4 fl oz milk, plus extra for glazing

1 egg, beaten

filling

675 g/1 lb 8 oz frozen or fresh cherries, pitted

300 g/10½ oz caster sugar, plus extra for sprinkling

2 tbsp gluten-free, wheat-free plain flour

3 tbsp gluten-free cornflour

juice and zest of 1 lemon

1. Preheat the oven to 190°C/375°F/Gas Mark 5. Grease a 12-hole muffin tray.

2. To make the pastry, sift the flour, xanthan gum and icing sugar into a large bowl. Rub in the butter using your fingertips until the mixture resembles fine breadcrumbs, then add the milk and egg (reserving some of the egg for glazing), and combine to make the pastry dough. Wrap the pastry in clingfilm and chill in the refrigerator for 30 minutes.

3. On a floured surface roll out the pastry to a thickness of 3 mm/⅛ inch and, using a 9-cm/ 3½-inch round cookie cutter, cut out 12 rounds to fit the prepared muffin tray. Press the pastry rounds into shape in the muffin tray.

4. In a bowl, combine the cherries, caster sugar, flour, cornflour and the juice and zest of the lemon. Divide the cherry mixture between the pastry cases. Roll out the remaining pastry and cut into 1 cm/½ inch wide strips and use to make a criss-cross lattice on top of the cherry filling, securing it at the edges with beaten egg.

5. Brush each pie with milk and sprinkle a little caster sugar on top. Bake in the preheated oven for 35–40 minutes until golden-brown on top. Remove from the oven and leave to cool in the tray for at least 1 hour before serving.

strawberry & vanilla cheesecake

Prep Time: 30 minutes   Cook Time: 50–60 minutes plus chilling
Per serving: 706 kcals/62g fat/38g saturated fat/33g carbs/15g sugar/1.3g salt

serves 12

biscuit base

300 g/10½ oz gluten-free, wheat-free digestive biscuits

200 g/7 oz butter, melted, plus extra for greasing

filling

900 g/2 lb cream cheese

115 g/4 oz caster sugar

3 tbsp gluten-free cornflour

3 eggs, beaten

100 ml/3½ fl oz double cream

450 g/1 lb strawberries, hulled

½ tsp vanilla essence

zest of 1 lemon

1. Preheat the oven to 200°C/400°F/Gas Mark 6. Grease a 23-cm/9-inch round springform cake tin and line the sides and bottom with baking paper.

2. Crush the biscuits using a food processor or place the biscuits in clingfilm or a polythene bag and crush them with a rolling pin.

3. Mix the butter and biscuit crumbs together and press into the bottom of the tin and bake in the preheated oven for 5 minutes. Remove from the oven and leave to cool.

4. Whisk the cream cheese, sugar and cornflour using a food processor or balloon whisk until light and creamy in consistency. Slowly add the eggs to the mixture and beat well. Slowly add the double cream to the mixture and beat until creamy.

5. Chop half the strawberries and add to the mixture with the vanilla essence and lemon zest.

6. Pour the mixture onto the biscuit base and bake in the preheated oven for 45–55 minutes or until the top is pale golden and the centre is set. Switch off the oven, leave the door ajar and leave until the cheesecake is cold – this prevents it from sinking. Chill in the refrigerator for at least 2 hours before serving. Release from the tin and decorate with the remaining fresh strawberries before serving.

key lime pie

Prep Time: 30 minutes   Cook Time: 30 minutes plus chilling
Per serving: 580 kcals/41g fat/23g saturated fat/50g carbs/32g sugar/0.8g salt

serves 10

biscuit base

300 g/10½ oz gluten-free digestive biscuits

50 g/1¾ oz caster sugar

140 g/5 oz butter, melted, plus extra for greasing

filling

4 egg yolks

410 ml/14½ fl oz condensed milk

juice of 6 limes (200 ml/7 fl oz in total)

finely grated zest of 4 limes

300 ml/10 fl oz double cream, to decorate

1. Preheat the oven to 180°C/350°F/Gas Mark 4. Grease a 22–24-cm/8½–9½-inch pie dish with melted butter.

2. Crush the biscuits using a food processor or place the biscuits in clingfilm or a polythene bag and crush them with a rolling pin. Mix the sugar, crushed biscuits and melted butter together in a large bowl.

3. Spread the crumb mixture over the base of the dish and up the sides, pressing firmly to pack it tight. Bake in the preheated oven for 10 minutes and then allow to cool.

4. To make the filling, whisk the egg yolks in a bowl and slowly add the condensed milk, whisking until creamy. Add the lime juice and zest, reserving some zest for decoration, and whip using a whisk.

5. Pour the mixture into the pie dish and bake in the preheated oven for 20 minutes or until the filling has firmed up with a slight wobble in the middle. Remove from the oven and allow to cool, then chill in the refrigerator for 3 hours.

6. When ready to serve, whip the double cream until it forms soft peaks, arrange small dollops of cream around the edge of the pie and decorate with the reserved lime zest.

pumpkin pie

Prep Time: 40 minutes plus chilling   Cook Time: 1–1¼ hours
Per serving: 316 kcals/22g fat/13g saturated fat/26g carbs/10.5g sugar/0.3g salt

serves 12

pastry

200 g/7 oz gluten-free, wheat-free plain flour, sifted, plus extra for dusting

25 g/1 oz rice flour

2 tbsp icing sugar

½ tsp xanthan gum

¼ tsp of salt

115 g/4 oz butter, plus extra for greasing

1 egg, beaten

2 tbsp cold water

filling

450 g/1 lb pumpkin, cut into chunks

2 eggs plus 1 egg yolk

300 ml/10 fl oz double cream

70 g/2½ oz brown sugar

1 tbsp maple syrup

1¼ tsp cinnamon

½ tsp ground cloves

½ tsp ginger

vanilla cream, to serve

1. Preheat the oven to 180°C/350°F/Gas Mark 4. Grease a 4-cm/1½-inch deep, 23-cm/9-inch fluted loose-based flan tin.

2. To make the pastry, place the flours, icing sugar, xanthan gum and salt in a mixing bowl. Add the butter and rub in with your fingertips until it resembles fine breadcrumbs.

3. Make a well in the centre of the mixture and add the egg and a little water. Using your hands, mix in the dry ingredients to form a dough. Turn the pastry out onto a floured surface and knead well. Wrap it in clingfilm and chill in the refrigerator for 20–30 minutes.

4. Roll out the pastry to a thickness of 3 mm/⅛ inch and use it to line the greased flan tin. Line the prepared pastry shell with baking paper and baking beans and bake blind in the preheated oven for 12 minutes until golden. Remove the baking paper and beans.

5. To make the filling, steam the pumpkin chunks for 20–25 minutes until tender. Drain and then purée in a food processor or blender.

6. Whisk the eggs and yolk in a bowl. Put the cream, brown sugar, maple syrup and spices in a pan and heat gently, being careful not to let them boil. Cool slightly, then add to the egg mixture and whisk together. Add the puréed pumpkin and mix well.

7. Pour the mixture into the pastry case and bake in the preheated oven for 30–35 minutes until firm to the touch. Remove from the oven and serve warm with vanilla cream.

3

4

7

pecan pie

Prep Time: 40 minutes plus chilling   Cook Time: 50–55 minutes
Per serving: 363 kcals/24g fat/8.5g saturated fat/33g carbs/17g sugar/0.4g salt

serves 12

pastry

200 g/7 oz gluten-free, wheat-free plain flour, sifted

25 g/1 oz rice flour

2 tbsp icing sugar

1/2 tsp xanthan gum

1/4 tsp of salt

115 g/4 oz butter, plus extra for greasing

1 egg, beaten

2 tbsp cold water

filling

115 g/4 oz caster sugar

3 large eggs

5 tbsp golden syrup

2 tbsp Bourbon

50 g/1 3/4 oz butter, melted

1/2 tsp vanilla essence

175 g/6 oz pecan halves

vanilla ice cream, to serve

1. Preheat the oven to 180°C/350°F/Gas Mark 4. Grease a 4-cm/1 1/2-inch deep, 23-cm/9-inch fluted loose-based flan tin.

2. Place the flours, icing sugar, xanthan gum and salt in a mixing bowl. Add the butter and rub in using your fingertips until it resembles fine breadcrumbs.

3. Make a well in the centre of the mixture and add the egg and a little water. Using your hands, mix in the dry ingredients to form a dough. Turn it out onto a floured surface and knead well. Wrap it in clingfilm and chill in the refrigerator for 20–30 minutes.

4. Roll out the pastry to a thickness of 3 mm/1/8 inch and use it to line the greased flan tin. Line the prepared pastry shell with baking paper and baking beans and bake blind in the preheated oven for 12 minutes until golden. Remove the baking paper and beans.

5. To make the filling, whisk the sugar and the eggs in a bowl. Slowly stir in the golden syrup, Bourbon, butter and vanilla essence. Scatter the pecans over the cooked pastry base. Pour the filling over the nuts and return to the oven. Bake for 35–40 minutes until just golden.

6. Remove from the oven. Serve warm or cold with vanilla ice cream.

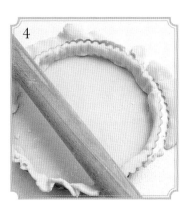

strawberry & vanilla cream profiteroles

Prep Time: 30 minutes   Cook Time: 25–30 minutes
Per serving: 953 kcals/78g fat/47g saturated fat/57g carbs/41g sugar/0.4g salt

serves 7

choux pastry

100 g/3½ oz butter

1 tsp caster sugar

300 ml/10 fl oz water

125 g/4½ oz gluten-free, wheat-free plain flour, sifted

4 eggs

cream filling

600 ml/1 pint double cream

1 tsp vanilla essence

225 g/8 oz strawberries, hulled and finely diced

chocolate sauce

50 g/1¾ oz caster sugar

150 ml/5 fl oz water

175 g/6 oz gluten-free plain chocolate, broken into pieces

15 g/½ oz butter

1. Preheat the oven to 200°C/400°F/Gas Mark 6. Line a baking tray with baking paper.

2. To make the choux pastry, heat the butter and sugar in a pan with the water and bring to the boil. Add the flour and remove from the heat. Mix with a wooden spoon until a dough ball forms. Leave the mixture to cool for 10–15 minutes.

3. When cool, beat in the eggs slowly until the dough is smooth and glossy. Spoon the dough into a piping bag fitted with a 2-cm/¾-inch plain nozzle and pipe about 35 small balls onto the baking tray. Each ball should be about the size of a walnut. Using a wet finger, rub the top of each ball to get rid of any lumps or bumps.

4. Bake in the preheated oven for 15–20 minutes until golden brown (if they are too pale they will go soggy). Remove from the oven and prick the base of each profiterole with a sharp skewer or knife to release the steam. Return to the baking tray with the hole facing upwards to dry out the centre for 5–6 minutes.

5. To make the filling, whip the double cream with the vanilla essence. Add the diced strawberries and stir. Spoon the mixture into a piping bag and pipe into the cooled profiteroles.

6. To make the chocolate sauce, heat the sugar and water in a small pan, stirring until dissolved. Bring to the boil, remove from the heat and add the chocolate pieces and butter, stir until melted and smooth.

7. Arrange the profiteroles on serving dishes and pour over the chocolate sauce. Serve immediately.

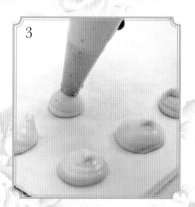

oven-baked chocolate & pistachio tart

Prep Time: 40 minutes plus chilling   Cook Time: 55–65 minutes plus chilling
Per serving: 480 kcals/29g fat/15g saturated fat/47g carbs/30g sugar/0.7g salt

serves 12

pastry

200 g/7 oz gluten-free, wheat-free plain flour

25 g/1 oz rice flour

2 tbsp icing sugar

½ tsp xanthan gum

¼ tsp of salt

115 g/4 oz butter, plus extra for greasing

1 egg, beaten

2 tbsp cold water

vanilla ice cream and strawberries, to serve

filling

150 g/5½ oz gluten-free dark chocolate, broken into pieces

140 g/5 oz butter

6 tbsp gluten-free cocoa powder

4 eggs

200 g/7 oz caster sugar

3 tbsp golden syrup

100 g/3½ oz roasted pistachio nuts, chopped

1. Preheat the oven to 150°C/300°F/Gas Mark 2. Grease a 4-cm/1½-inch deep, 23-cm/9-inch fluted loose-based flan tin.

2. To make the pastry, sift the flours, icing sugar, xanthan gum and salt into a mixing bowl. Add the butter and rub in using your fingertips until the mixture resembles fine breadcrumbs.

3. Make a well in the centre of the mixture and add the egg and a little water. Using your hands, mix in the dry ingredients to form a dough. Turn it out onto a floured surface and knead well. Wrap it in clingfilm and chill in the refrigerator for 20–30 minutes.

4. Roll the pastry out to a thickness of 3 mm/⅛ inch and use it to line the greased flan tin. Line the prepared pastry shell with baking paper and baking beans and bake blind in the preheated oven for 12 minutes until golden. Remove the baking paper and beans.

5. To make the filling, melt the chocolate, butter and cocoa powder in a heatproof bowl set over a saucepan of simmering water, stirring continuously.

6. In a bowl whisk the eggs, sugar and golden syrup together until light and creamy. Then add the chocolate mixture and pistachio nuts, and mix well.

7. Fill the tart case with the chocolate and pistachio mixture and bake in the preheated oven for 40–50 minutes. Remove from the oven and allow to cool for approximately 30–60 minutes. Serve with vanilla ice cream and strawberries.

lemon meringue pie

Prep Time: 45 minutes plus chilling   Cook Time: 30–35 minutes
Per serving: 415 kcals/19g fat/10g saturated fat/60g carbs/36g sugar/0.5g salt

serves 12

pastry

200 g/7 oz gluten-free,
wheat-free plain flour,
sifted

25 g/1 oz rice flour

2 tbsp icing sugar

$\frac{1}{2}$ tsp xanthan gum

$\frac{1}{4}$ tsp of salt

115 g/4 oz butter

1 egg, beaten

2 tbsp cold water

lemon filling

juice and zest of 4 lemons

100 g/3$\frac{1}{2}$ oz caster sugar

6 tbsp gluten-free cornflour

6 egg yolks

100 g/3$\frac{1}{2}$ oz butter

meringue

6 egg whites

1 tsp gluten-free cornflour

$\frac{1}{2}$ tsp white wine vinegar

300 g/10$\frac{1}{2}$ oz caster sugar

1. Preheat the oven to 150°C/300°F/Gas Mark 2. Grease a 4-cm/1$\frac{1}{2}$-inch deep, 23-cm/9-inch fluted loose-based flan tin.

2. Sift the flours, icing sugar, xanthan gum and salt into a mixing bowl. Add the butter and rub in with your fingertips until it resembles fine breadcrumbs. Make a well in the centre of the mixture and add the egg and a little water. Using your hands, mix in the dry ingredients to form a dough. Turn the pastry out onto a floured surface and knead well. Wrap it in clingfilm and chill in the refrigerator for 20–30 minutes.

3. Roll the pastry out to a thickness of 3 mm/$\frac{1}{8}$ inch and use it to line the greased flan tin. Line the prepared pastry shell with baking paper and baking beans and bake blind in the preheated oven for 12 minutes until golden. Remove the baking paper and beans.

4. To make the filling, measure the lemon juice and make up to 300 ml/10 fl oz with water. Tip into a pan with the lemon zest and sugar and bring to the boil. Mix the cornflour to a paste with a little water, add to the hot lemon mix and simmer, stirring continuously for 1 minute until the mixture has boiled and thickened. Remove from the heat, and cool for 5 minutes. Gradually add the egg yolks and butter, beating well between additions. Pour the mixture into the pastry case and leave until cold and set. Increase the oven temperature to 180°C/350°F/Gas Mark 4.

5. To make the meringue, whisk the egg whites, cornflour and vinegar in a bowl until it forms stiff peaks. Slowly add the sugar, whisking until the meringue is stiff and glossy.

6. Pipe or spoon the meringue on top of the lemon pie, ensuring the meringue goes right to the edge. Bake in the preheated oven for 10–15 minutes until golden brown. Remove from the oven and serve warm or cool.

old-fashioned apple pie

Prep Time: 45 minutes plus chilling   Cook Time: 45–50 minutes
Per serving: 464 kcals/15g fat/9g saturated fat/80g carbs/36g sugar/0.8g salt

serves 8

pastry

450 g/1 lb gluten-free, wheat-free self-raising flour, plus extra for dusting

1/2 tsp xanthan gum

40 g/1 1/2 oz icing sugar

125 g/4 1/2 oz butter, plus extra for greasing

1 egg, plus extra for glazing

125 ml/4 fl oz milk, plus extra for glazing

ice cream or hot custard sauce, to serve

filling

7–8 cooking apples, cored, peeled and sliced

100 g/3 1/2 oz caster sugar, plus extra for sprinkling

1 tsp gluten-free cornflour

2 tbsp water

1 tsp cinnamon

2 cloves

1. Preheat the oven to 180°C/350°F/Gas Mark 4. Grease a 20–25-cm/8–10-inch ovenproof pie dish.

2. To make the filling, put the sliced apple, caster sugar, cornflour, water, cinnamon and cloves into a pan and cook until the apple is just tender. Drain the apple mix in a sieve and leave to cool.

3. To make the pastry, sift the flour, xanthan gum and icing sugar into a large bowl. Rub in the butter with your fingertips until the mixture resembles fine breadcrumbs. Add the egg and milk and combine to make the pastry dough. Wrap in clingfilm and chill in the refrigerator for 20 minutes.

4. On a floured surface, divide the pastry in two and roll each piece out to form a large round – one to line the pie dish and one to go on top of the pie. Line the pie dish with one of the pastry rounds and add the apple filling.

5. Mix together a little milk and egg and brush the rim of the pastry with this. Add the second pastry round as a lid and, using a fork, crimp the edges of the pastry all the way around. Pierce the pie in the middle a couple of times to let out steam during baking. Use any leftover pastry to decorate the top of the pie.

6. Brush the top of the pie with milk and egg mixture and sprinkle with caster sugar. Bake in the preheated oven for 35–40 minutes until golden.

7. Remove from the oven and sprinkle with a little more caster sugar and serve with ice cream or hot custard sauce.

Chapter 5
Breads & Savoury Pastries

...rain bread

...rising   Cook Time: 40–45 minutes
...turated fat/383g carbs/31g sugar/1.7g salt

...utter, for greasing

60 g/2¼ oz amaranth flour

120 g/4¼ oz brown rice flour

120 g/4¼ oz sorghum flour

60 g/2¼ oz gluten-free cornflour

60 g/2¼ oz tapioca flour

20 g/¾ oz ground chia seeds

100 g/3½ oz ground flax seeds

2 tsp xanthan gum

2 tsp easy-blend dried yeast

1 tsp salt

3 eggs

1 tbsp vegetable oil

2 tbsp sugar

240 ml/8½ fl oz tepid water

10 g/¼ oz sunflower seeds

1. Grease a 450-g/1-lb loaf tin.

2. Combine the flours, chia seeds, flax seeds, xanthan gum, yeast and salt together in a bowl.

3. In a separate bowl, mix the eggs, vegetable oil, sugar and water together until well combined. Add the dry ingredients to the egg mixture and mix well to form a soft dough.

4. Put the dough into the prepared tin, sprinkle with the sunflower seeds and cover with a clean damp tea towel. Leave in a warm place for an hour until the dough rises. Preheat the oven to 180°C/350°F/Gas Mark 4.

5. Remove the tea towel and bake the loaf in the preheated oven for 40–45 minutes until golden brown. Remove from the oven and allow to cool in the tin. When cooled, remove from the tin.

white bread rolls

Prep Time: 30 minutes plus rising   Cook Time: 20–25 minutes
Per roll: 184 kcals/4g fat/1g saturated fat/33g carbs/3g sugar/0.3g salt

makes 24

4 eggs

4 tbsp vegetable oil

60 g/2¼ oz caster sugar

1 tbsp xanthan gum

85 g/3 oz potato flour

480 g/1 lb 1 oz white rice flour, plus extra for dusting

250 g/9 oz tapioca flour

85 g/3 oz buckwheat flour

3 tsp easy-blend dried yeast

1 tsp salt

300 ml/10 fl oz tepid milk

1. Preheat the oven to 190°C/375°F/Gas Mark 5. Line 1–2 baking trays with baking paper.

2. Combine the eggs, vegetable oil and sugar in a large bowl and mix well using a food processor or hand whisk.

3. Add the xanthan gum, potato flour, white rice flour, tapioca flour, buckwheat flour, yeast and salt and combine well, gradually adding the tepid milk until a thick bread dough is formed.

4. Transfer the dough from the bowl to a floured surface and knead for 1–2 minutes. Divide and shape the dough into 24 balls, using extra flour if necessary to prevent the dough from sticking.

5. Place the rolls on the baking tray, cover with a clean damp tea towel and leave them to rise at room temperature for 45–60 minutes until they have almost doubled in size.

6. Bake in the preheated oven for 20–25 minutes until golden brown. Remove from the oven and cool on a wire rack.

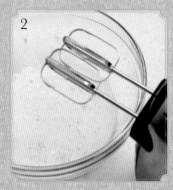

mixed grain bread

Prep Time: 40 minutes plus rising   Cook Time: 30 minutes
Per loaf: 3697 kcals/179g fat/19g saturated fat/417g carbs/16g sugar/5.8g salt

makes 1 loaf

butter, for greasing

2½ tsp dried yeast

425 ml/15 fl oz tepid water

1 tbsp maple syrup

120 g/4¼ oz gluten-free oat flour

175 g/6 oz rice flour

175 g/6 oz almond flour

120 g/4¼ oz buckwheat flour

20 g/¾ oz tapioca flour

60 g/2¼ oz quinoa flour

1 tsp xanthan gum

1 tsp salt

3 eggs, beaten

4 tbsp sunflower oil

1 tbsp gluten-free porridge oats

1. Grease and line a 900-g/2-lb loaf tin with baking paper.

2. Mix the yeast with 125 ml/4 fl oz of the warm water and add the maple syrup. Mix well and leave at room temperature for 10–15 minutes until frothy.

3. Mix all the flours, xanthan gum and salt in a large bowl. Make a well in the middle of the mixture and add the yeast liquid.

4. Add the eggs and the sunflower oil and mix together, adding the remaining water a little at a time to form a firm dough. Turn out onto a lightly floured surface and knead for about 5 minutes until smooth and elastic.

5. Shape the loaf and place in the tin. Brush with a little water then scatter over the oats. Cover with a clean damp tea towel and leave in a warm place until the loaf has risen and is twice its size.

6. Preheat the oven to 180°C/350°F/Gas Mark 4. Bake in the preheated oven for 30 minutes or until golden and crusty. Cool in the tin for 5 minutes then turn out onto a wire rack to cool completely.

2

3

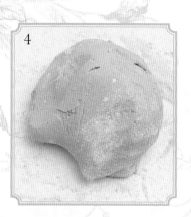

4

caramelised red onion, thyme & olive focaccia bread

Prep Time: 30 minutes plus rising   Cook Time: 30–35 minutes
Per loaf: 2586 kcals/88g fat/45g saturated fat/393g carbs/44g sugar/7.5g salt

makes 1 loaf

butter, for greasing

450 g/1 lb gluten-free, wheat-free white bread flour

2 tsp dried yeast

2 tsp caster sugar

350 ml/12 fl oz tepid milk

2 eggs, beaten

1 garlic clove, finely chopped

10–12 black olives, stoned and halved

rock salt

cracked black pepper

grated Parmesan cheese, for sprinkling

caramelised onion

50 g/1¾ oz butter

2 small red onions, thinly sliced

4–5 sprigs thyme

1. To make the caramelised onion, melt the butter in a small frying pan and fry the onion and thyme gently until the onion is soft and caramelised. Remove from the heat and cool until required.

2. Grease a 25- x 35-cm/10- x 14-inch baking tray and line with baking paper.

3. Sift the flour into a bowl. In a separate bowl, mix the yeast, sugar and tepid milk and leave to stand for 5–10 minutes at room temperature until frothy. Mix in the eggs and add the liquid mixture to the flour and mix well.

4. Transfer the dough onto the prepared tray, pushing it out to the edges. Cover with a clean damp tea towel and leave for about 45 minutes until it has doubled in size. Preheat the oven to 180°C/350°F/Gas Mark 4.

5. Spread the caramelised onion over the top of the bread, sprinkle with the garlic, olives, salt, pepper and Parmesan. Press the toppings lightly into the bread using your fingers.

6. Bake in the preheated oven for 30–35 minutes until golden and crusty. Remove from the oven and leave to cool on a wire rack. The bread can be served hot or cold.

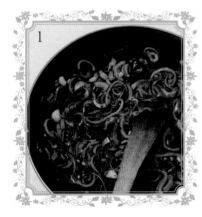

mexican-style tortilla wraps

Prep Time: 15–20 minutes   Cook Time: 5–6 minutes per wrap
Per tortilla: 160 kcals/3g fat/0.5g saturated fat/31g carbs/0.6g sugar/trace salt

makes 10

10 g/¼ oz dried yeast

400 ml/14 fl oz tepid water

2 tbsp sunflower oil

400 g/14 oz gluten-free, wheat-free plain flour, plus extra for dusting

1½ tsp xanthan gum

2 tbsp chopped coriander (optional)

½ tsp chilli flakes (optional)

salt and pepper

1. Mix the yeast, tepid water and oil in a jug and leave at room temperature for approximately 20 minutes until frothy.

2. Sift the flour and xanthan gum into a large bowl and make a well in the centre. Add the yeast liquid to the well slowly with the coriander, chilli, if using, salt and pepper. Mix well to form a sticky dough.

3. Turn out onto a floured surface and knead well. Divide into 8–10 small balls.

4. Cut out a circle of baking paper 20 cm/8 inches in diameter and roll out each ball of dough under this, the thinner the better.

5. Place a non-stick pan on a medium heat. Add the tortillas to the pan, one at a time, with the baking paper underneath and cook for 2–3 minutes until golden brown. Flip over, remove the paper and cook the other side for 2–3 minutes until golden brown. If the paper starts to scorch, cut a new circle.

6. Serve hot or cold with your favourite fillings. To store, divide each tortilla with baking paper to prevent sticking and keep in an airtight container for up to 1 week or freeze for 1–2 months.

pizza base

Prep Time: 30–40 minutes   Cook Time: 25 minutes
Per base: 353 kcals/5.5g fat/1g saturated fat/65g carbs/5g sugar/1.5g salt

makes 4 bases

225 ml/8 fl oz tepid water

30 g/1 oz dried milk

1 tsp sugar

3 tsp dried yeast

125 g/4½ oz gluten-free, wheat-free bread flour, sifted, plus extra for dusting

175 g/6 oz rice flour

2 tsp gluten-free baking powder

1 tsp salt

½ tsp xanthan gum

1 egg

1 tbsp sunflower oil

pizza sauce and toppings of your choice, to serve

1. Place the tepid water in a bowl and dissolve the dried milk, sugar and yeast in it. Leave to stand at room temperature for approximately 5–10 minutes until frothy.

2. In a large bowl, mix the bread flour, rice flour, baking powder, salt and xanthan gum together.

3. In a separate bowl, whisk the egg and sunflower oil together and then add to the dry mixture. Pour in the yeast liquid and continue to mix until a soft dough forms.

4. On a floured surface roll out the dough and divide into four balls of equal size. Cut out 4 circles of baking paper 20 cm/8 inches in diameter and roll out the dough to fit each circle. Cover the pizza bases with a clean damp tea towel for 10–15 minutes before baking. Preheat the oven to 200°C/400°F/Gas Mark 6.

5. Place the pizza bases, with the baking paper, on a baking tray and bake in the preheated oven for 10 minutes.

6. Remove from the oven, add your pizza sauce and favourite toppings and return to the oven and bake for another 10–15 minutes.

pear, oat & blueberry breakfast loaf

Prep Time: 30 minutes   Cook Time: 55 minutes–1 hour
Per loaf: 2982 kcals/114g fat/61g saturated fat/471g carbs/287g sugar/6.9g salt

makes 1 loaf

200 g/7 oz caster sugar

100 g/3½ oz butter, plus extra for greasing

2 large eggs, beaten

½ tsp vanilla essence

125 g/4½ oz gluten-free, wheat-free plain flour, sifted

1 tsp gluten-free baking powder

½ tsp gluten-free bicarbonate of soda

¼ tsp xanthan gum

85 g/3 oz gluten-free, wheat-free oats, plus extra for sprinkling

pinch of salt

½ tsp ground cinnamon

3 bananas, mashed

4 tbsp milk

2 cooked or canned pear halves, diced

70 g/2½ oz blueberries

demerara sugar, for sprinkling

1. Preheat the oven to 180°C/350°F/Gas Mark 4. Grease a 900-g/2-lb loaf tin and line with baking paper.

2. Cream the sugar and butter in a bowl. Add the eggs and vanilla essence slowly.

3. In a separate bowl, mix the flour, baking powder, bicarbonate of soda, xanthan gum, oats, salt and cinnamon together and then add to the egg mixture. Add the mashed banana and milk and mix well until combined.

4. Spoon half of the mix into the prepared loaf tin and then sprinkle with the diced pear and two-thirds of the blueberries. Spoon the remaining sponge mixture on top. Scatter over the remaining blueberries, the oats and the demerara sugar.

5. Bake in the preheated oven for 55 minutes–1 hour, or until a skewer inserted comes out clean. Remove from the oven and leave to cool in the tin.

deep-filled chicken & oyster mushroom pie

Prep Time: 30 minutes plus chilling   Cook Time: 45–55 minutes
Per serving: 641 kcals/42g fat/25g saturated fat/39g carbs/4.5g sugar/1.1g salt

serves 6

pastry

225 g/8 oz gluten-free wheat-free plain white flour

25 g/1 oz Parmesan cheese, grated

½ tsp xanthan gum

pinch of salt

125 g/4½ oz butter

1 egg, beaten

filling

50 g/1¾ oz butter

1 small white onion, diced

280 g/10 oz mushrooms, chopped

175 g/6 oz oyster mushrooms, torn into strips

2 tsp crushed garlic

3 tbsp gluten-free, wheat-free plain flour

320 ml/11 fl oz milk

juice of 1 lime

160 ml/5½ fl oz crème fraîche

2 tsp dried tarragon

450 g/1 lb fresh cooked chicken, chopped into large chunks

1 egg yolk, beaten

salt and pepper

1. Preheat the oven to 180°C/350°F/Gas Mark 4. Grease a 7-cm/3-inch deep, 23- x 27-cm/9- x 10¾-inch pie dish.

2. Place the flour, Parmesan cheese, xanthan gum and salt into a bowl. Add the butter and rub in with your fingertips until it resembles fine breadcrumbs. Make a well in the centre of the mixture and add the egg and a little water. Using your hands, mix in the dry ingredients to form a dough. Turn it out onto a floured surface and knead well. Wrap it in clingfilm and chill in the refrigerator for 20–30 minutes.

3. To make the filling, melt the butter in a small pan and fry the onion and mushrooms gently until soft. Add the garlic and season to taste with salt and pepper. Add the flour and cook for 2–3 minutes, mixing the flour through the mushroom mixture.

4. Remove the pan from the heat and slowly add the milk. When all the milk has been added, put the pan back on the heat and stir well, until the sauce bubbles and becomes smooth. Cook for 2–3 minutes on a low heat and then set aside. Add the lime juice, crème fraîche, tarragon and cooked chicken to the cooling mixture.

5. Place a pie funnel in the centre of the pie dish, then spoon in the filling around it. Roll out the pastry and cut an oval slightly larger than the top of the pie. Slice the trimmings into 1-cm/ ½-inch wide strips and attach them to the rim of the pie dish, using a little water. Brush these edges with water then lift the pastry on top of the pie. Trim the edges, then seal and crimp the pastry. Make a cut so the top of the funnel sticks out of the pastry. Use any leftover pastry to decorate the top of the pie. Brush the top of the pie with the beaten egg yolk and make a couple of slits in the top with a sharp knife to allow the steam to escape.

6. Bake in the preheated oven for 30–40 minutes until the pastry is golden and flaky. Serve immediately. As an alternative, the pie could be topped with cheesy mashed potato instead of the pastry.

1

4

4

roast tomato, asparagus & gruyère cheese quiche

Prep Time: 30 minutes plus chilling   Cook Time: 40–45 minutes
Per serving: 466 kcals/37g fat/21g saturated fat/24g carbs/2g sugar/0.8g salt

serves 8

pastry

225 g/8 oz gluten-free, wheat-free plain flour, plus extra for dusting

½ tsp xanthan gum

½ tsp salt

115 g/4 oz butter, plus extra for greasing

1 egg, beaten

4 tbsp water

filling

8–10 asparagus stems

3 eggs plus 1 egg yolk

250 ml/9 fl oz double cream

1 shallot, diced

100 g/3½ oz Gruyère cheese, grated

1 tbsp snipped chives

1 tbsp flat-leaf parsley, chopped

12–14 cherry tomatoes

salt and pepper

1. Grease a 4-cm/1½-inch deep, 23-cm/9-inch fluted loose-based flan tin.

2. To make the pastry, place the flour, xanthan gum and salt into a bowl. Add the butter and rub in with your fingertips until it resembles fine breadcrumbs.

3. Make a well in the centre of the mixture and add the egg and a little water. Using your hands, mix in the dry ingredients to form a dough. Turn it out onto a floured surface and knead well. Wrap it in clingfilm and chill in the refrigerator for 20–30 minutes.

4. Roll out the pastry on a floured surface and use it to line the prepared flan tin. Place in the freezer for 20 minutes. Preheat the oven to 180°C/350°F/Gas Mark 4.

5. Remove the pastry from the freezer, line with baking paper and baking beans and bake blind in the preheated oven for 10 minutes. Remove the baking paper and beans and allow the pastry to cool slightly before adding the filling.

6. To make the filling, cut the asparagus stems in half. Cook in boiling salted water for 3 minutes or until just tender. Drain, rinse in cold water and drain again. Beat the eggs, egg yolk and cream together with salt and pepper. Scatter the shallot, half the cheese and half the chives and parsley over the pastry base. Top with the blanched asparagus, cherry tomatoes and remaining cheese and herbs. Pour over the egg mixture.

7. Return the quiche to the oven, reduce the temperature to 160°C/325°F/Gas Mark 3 and bake for 25–30 minutes or until the top is golden and the filling set. Serve warm or cool.

individual chicken & ham pot pies

Prep Time: 45 minutes plus chilling   Cook Time: 1¾–2¼ hours
Per pie: 1011 kcals/63g fat/37g saturated fat/56g carbs/3g sugar/2.7g salt

serves 6

pastry

450 g/1 lb gluten-free, wheat-free plain flour, plus extra for dusting

40 g/1½ oz Parmesan cheese, grated

½ tsp xanthan gum

½ tsp salt

220 g/7¾ oz butter, plus extra for greasing

2 eggs, beaten

filling

1 whole chicken, 1.8 kg/4 lb in weight

1 leek, chopped

1 garlic clove

2 thyme sprigs

360 ml/12½ fl oz double cream

4 tbsp gluten-free, wheat-free plain flour

4 tbsp butter, softened

400 g/14 oz mushrooms, washed and halved

450 g/1 lb cooked ham, chopped into large chunks

200 g/7 oz sweetcorn

2 spring onions, chopped

3 tbsp chopped chives

salt and pepper

buttered greens and mashed potato, to serve

1. Place the chicken in a large saucepan with the leek, garlic and thyme and cover with water. Bring to the boil, reduce the heat, cover and simmer for 1 hour–1 hour 20 minutes until the chicken is tender and the juices run clear when a skewer is inserted into the thickest part of the meat. Remove the chicken from the pot and cool. Simmer the remaining stock down to 850 ml/1½ pints.

2. Preheat the oven to 180°C/350°F/Gas Mark 4. Grease six individual 400-ml/14-fl oz pie dishes.

3. To make the pastry, place the flour, Parmesan cheese, xanthan gum and salt into a bowl. Add the butter and rub in with your fingertips until it resembles fine breadcrumbs. Make a well in the centre of the mixture and add the eggs (reserving some of the egg for glazing) and a little water. Using your hands, mix in the dry ingredients to form a dough. Turn it out onto a floured surface and knead well. Wrap the dough in clingfilm and chill in the refrigerator for 20–30 minutes.

4. To make the sauce, add the cream to the reserved chicken stock and bring to the boil. Mix the equal quantities of flour and butter together and then gradually add it to the boiling stock, whisking well until the sauce thickens. Remove from the heat and leave to cool. Chop the cooked chicken roughly and add to the sauce with the mushrooms, ham, sweetcorn, onions and chives and season to taste. Divide the mixture between the prepared pie dishes.

5. Roll out the pastry and cut out 6 ovals slightly larger than the top of the pie dishes. Slice the trimmings into 1-cm/½-inch wide strips and attach them to the rims of the dishes, using a little water. Brush these edges with water then lift the pastry tops onto the pies. Trim the edges, then seal and crimp the pastry and brush with a little beaten egg. Make a couple of slits in the top with a sharp knife to allow the steam to escape.

6. Bake in the preheated oven for 30–40 minutes until golden. Remove from the oven and serve with buttered greens and mashed potato.

Breads & Savoury Pastries 157

almonds 17
  Almond & Pear Crunch Cake 108
  Almond & Pistachio Biscotti 62
  Carrot Cupcakes with Almond & Lime
    Frosting 26
amaranth 16
Angel Food Cake 88
apples
  Apple & Cinnamon Bran Muffins 36
  Country-style Farmhouse Fruit Cake 74
  Old-fashioned Apple Pie 134
  Pear & Apple Oat Crisp 104
apricots
  Apricot & Coconut Bars 48
  Apricot, Cranberry & Chocolate Chip
    Flapjacks 66
  Country-style Farmhouse Fruit Cake 74
  Drambuie Christmas Cake 96
arrowroot 16
asparagus
  Roast Tomato, Asparagus & Gruyère
    Cheese Quiche 154

bananas
  Banana Bread 84
  Banana Muffins with Maple Cream
    Frosting 28
  Chocolate & Walnut Banana Bread 80
  Upside-down Banana & Maple Syrup
    Cake 110
bars
  Apricot & Coconut Bars 48
  Breakfast Cereal Bars 52
  Chewy Chocolate & Mixed
    Berry Bars 50
  Rocky Road Snack Bars 54
berries
  Chewy Chocolate & Mixed
    Berry Bars 50
biscotti
  Almond & Pistachio Biscotti 62
Black Forest Gateau 90
blackberries
  Rhubarb & Blackberry Crumble 106
blueberries
  Blueberry & Oatmeal Muffins 32
  Pear, Oat & Blueberry Breakfast
    Loaf 150

bran
  Apple & Cinnamon Bran Muffins 36
brandy
  Glazed Brandy & Date Bread & Butter
    Pudding 112
bread
  Banana Bread 84
  Bread & Butter Pudding, Glazed
    Brandy & Date 112
  Chocolate & Walnut Banana
    Bread 80
  Caramelised Red Onion, Thyme &
    Olive Focaccia Bread 144
  Courgette Bread 86
  Mixed Grain Bread 142
  Seven Grain Bread 138
  White Bread Rolls 140
Breakfast Cereal Bars 52
brown rice flour 16
brownies
  Hazelnut & White Chocolate
    Brownies 64
buckwheat 16
Buttermilk & Sultana Scones 42

cakes
  Almond & Pear Crunch Cake 108
  Angel Food Cake 88
  Black Forest Gateau 90
  Carrot Cake with Lemon Cream
    Frosting 70
  Chocolate & Raspberry Gateau 92
  Chocolate Fudge Cake 72
  Country-style Farmhouse Fruit Cake 74
  Drambuie Christmas Cake 96
  Lemon Zest Birthday Cake 98
  Pumpkin & Walnut Cake 100
  Sticky Fruit Loaf 82
  Upside-down Banana & Maple Syrup
    Cake 110
  Victoria Sponge with Vanilla Cream &
    Strawberries 78
  Caramelised Red Onion, Thyme & Olive
    Focaccia Bread 144
  Carrot Cake with Lemon Cream
    Frosting 70
  Carrot Cupcakes with Almond & Lime
    Frosting 26

cheese
  Roast Tomato, Asparagus & Gruyère
    Cheese Quiche 154
cheesecake
  Strawberry & Vanilla Cheesecake 120
  White Chocolate & Irish Cream
    Cheesecake 116
cherries
  Black Forest Gateau 90
  Drambuie Christmas Cake 96
  Mini Cherry Pies 118
chestnuts 17
Chewy Chocolate & Mixed
    Berry Bars 50
chia 16
chicken
  Deep-filled Chicken & Oyster
    Mushroom Pie 152
  Individual Chicken & Ham Pot Pies 156
chocolate
  Apricot, Cranberry & Chocolate Chip
    Flapjacks 66
  Black Forest Gateau 90
  Chewy Chocolate & Mixed
    Berry Bars 50
  Chocolate & Macadamia Nut
    Cupcakes 24
  Chocolate & Raspberry Gateau 92
  Chocolate & Vanilla Whoopie Pies 38
  Chocolate & Walnut Banana Bread 80
  Chocolate Fudge Cake 72
  Fudge Frosted Chocolate Muffins 30
  Hazelnut & White Chocolate
    Brownies 64
  Mandarin & Chocolate Chip
    Cookies 58
  Mocha Bundt Cake 76
  Oatmeal & Vanilla Cookies 60
  Oven-baked Chocolate & Pistachio
    Tart 130
  Oven-baked Soft-centred Chocolate
    Pudding 114
  Raspberry & White Chocolate
    Cupcakes 22
  Rocky Road Cake Pops 40
  Rocky Road Snack Bars 54
  Strawberry & Vanilla Cream
    Profiteroles 128
  Vanilla, Cinnamon & Chocolate
    Doughnuts 44
  White Chocolate & Irish Cream
    Cheesecake 116